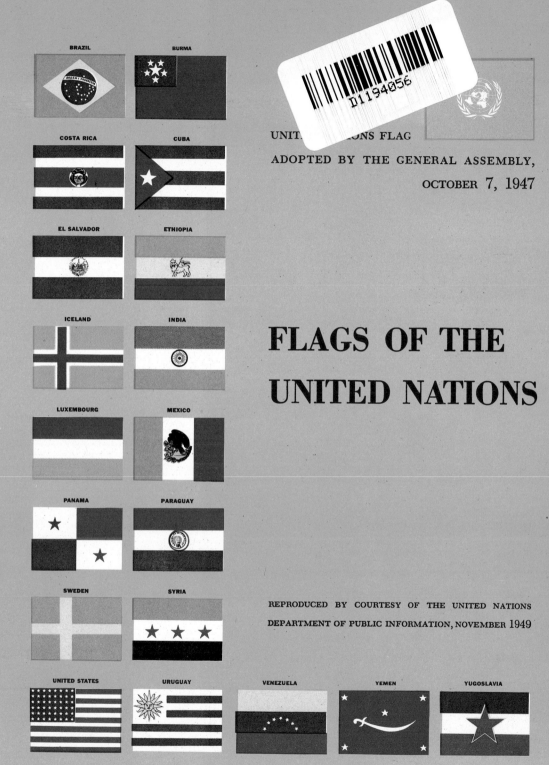

UNITED NATIONS FLAG

ADOPTED BY THE GENERAL ASSEMBLY,

OCTOBER 7, 1947

FLAGS OF THE
UNITED NATIONS

REPRODUCED BY COURTESY OF THE UNITED NATIONS
DEPARTMENT OF PUBLIC INFORMATION, NOVEMBER 1949

PARTNERS
The United Nations and Youth

PARTNERS

The United Nations and Youth

BY ELEANOR ROOSEVELT AND HELEN FERRIS

DOUBLEDAY & CO., INC.
Garden City, New York

GUATEMALA INDIANS
TRANSPORT UNICEF FOOD TO
THE YOUTH OF A REMOTE VILLAGE

TEEN-AGE
VISITORS ADMIRING THE BEAUTIFUL
NEW UNITED NATIONS BUILDING
ON THE EAST RIVER IN NEW YORK CITY

ABOUT THIS BOOK

This book really had its start in the times my husband talked with me of his hopes and dreams for the United Nations that was to be. It was always of the people that he spoke then, the people of the world working together in their international organization. For he loved people, and he believed in them.

So often, as the stories here have come in, I have wished I might share these young people with him. He would have been so pleased that Arturo's skim-milk problem was solved. He would have understood so well teen-age Kyria's rebellion as she kicked over the children's playhouse. He would have had more than one chuckle over Aunt Kuo and her charges. And for Frankie and his roller-skating triumph, he would have had a special, personal understanding.

It was difficult for Helen Ferris and me to choose from among the many stories in the letters and field reports, the UN radio scripts, articles, and interviews so generously given us. We wished to include them all! But since a single book could not possibly do that, we tried to select those typical of the great partnership of youth and their United Nations, typical of the way in which the UN itself works.

We are most grateful to those who found the stories for us, who gave us intimate glimpses of just how they are doing their work in the UN. And we are grateful to the young people themselves for being themselves.

Eleanor Roosevelt

Hyde Park, New York
August 1950

THIS PRIZE-WINNING
POSTER IN UNESCO'S
INTERNATIONAL
CONTEST FOR YOUTH
WAS PAINTED BY
FRANCINE JACOBS
OF BELGIUM

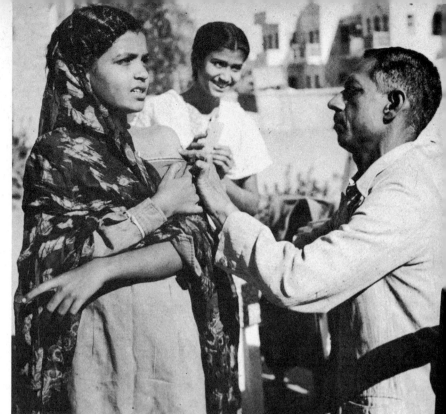

EVERYONE
HAS THE RIGHT
TO GOOD HEALTH
— A PAKISTAN
WHO DOCTOR
VACCINATES A
STUDENT IN THE
NEWTOWN GIRLS'
SCHOOL, KARACHI

CONTENTS

About this book BY ELEANOR ROOSEVELT, 5

A Pledge to Youth   17
For Thérèse, Pierre, and the Others   35
The Same in Every Language   45
The Teams Arrive   61
Bread is Peace   77
On Call Day and Night   93
A Bridge of Friendship   109
Living and Learning Together   131
The Peoples Speak with the Peoples   145
Without Boundaries   157
Human Rights   179

In Appreciation, 189
Bibliography, 193
Index, 201

UNITED
NATIONS
FLAGS
FEATURE
A GIRL SCOUT
CONFERENCE

UNITED NATIONS INITIALS

ECE	*Economic Commission for Europe*
ESC	*Economic and Social Council*
FAO	*Food and Agriculture Organization*
GA	*General Assembly*
ICAO	*International Civil Aviation Organization*
ICJ	*International Court of Justice*
ILO	*International Labor Organization*
IRO	*International Refugee Organization*
SC	*Security Council*
TC	*Trusteeship Council*
UNESCO	*United Nations Educational, Scientific and Cultural Organization*
UNICEF	*United Nations International Children's Emergency Fund*
UPU	*Universal Postal Union*
WHO	*World Health Organization*

MANY FRENCH YOUNG
PEOPLE WERE AMONG
THE HUNDREDS OF VISITORS
AT UNESCO'S HUMAN
RIGHTS EXHIBITION IN PARIS

PHOTOGRAPHS AND CREDITS

2 *Guatemala Indians transport UNICEF food to the youth of a remote village.* UNICEF PHOTO

5 *Youthful visitors to the new UN building, New York City.* UNICEF PHOTO

6 *Prize-winning poster in UNESCO'S international contest.* UNESCO PHOTO

7 *A Pakistan doctor vaccinating students in Karachi.* UNICEF PHOTO

8 *United Nations flags at Girl Scout Conference.* NATIONAL GIRL SCOUT PHOTO

9 *French young people at the Paris Human Rights Exhibition.* UNESCO PHOTO

14 *Malayan school children in Kampong Bagan Blat gather for mid-morning milk.* UNICEF PHOTO

16 *The new UN building during construction, New York City.* UN PHOTO

17 *A war orphan arrives in the United States.* IRO PHOTO

23 *A typical DP refugee center.* IRO PHOTO

23 *Boarding an IRO chartered ship.* IRO PHOTO

23 *The 150,000th DP enters the United States.* IRO PHOTO

29 *DP girls learning sewing.* IRO PHOTO

29 *DP boys learning toolmaking.* IRO PHOTO

29 *Singing time in a DP center.* IRO PHOTO

29 *Story Hour in a DP center.* AMERICAN FRIENDS SERVICE COMMITTEE
     PHOTO

35 *A typical UNICEF shipment.* UNICEF PHOTO

39 *Milk time at a feeding center.* UNICEF PHOTO

44 *Trygve Lie welcomes a Finnish student.* UN PHOTO

45 *Blankets arrive in Macedonia.* UNICEF PHOTO

49 *A roadside feeding station in Greece.* UNICEF PHOTO

49 *Mealtime for young Palestine refugees.* UNICEF PHOTO

55 *A teen-age Italian orphan girl makes a dress.* UNICEF PHOTO

55 *A teen-age Greek boy makes shoes.* UNICEF PHOTO

59 *Camels delivering skim-milk powder in Palestine.* UNICEF PHOTO

60 *A Bolivian mother takes her baby to a clinic.* BOLIVIAN EMBASSY PHOTO

61 *A Danish nurse and Czechoslovakian boy.* UNICEF PHOTO

65 *A BCG car in Yugoslavia.* UNICEF PHOTO

65 *A Serbian woman doctor and girl helpers.* UNICEF PHOTO

69 *College girls in India taking TB test.* UNICEF PHOTO

69 *French doctors and Tunisian youth.* UNICEF PHOTO

73 *Milk time in a Guatemala school.* UNICEF PHOTO

73   *Lunch time in a Tokyo school.* UNICEF PHOTO

75   *Yugoslavian girls sing a welcome to UNICEF friends.* UNICEF PHOTO

76   *A Greek nutritionist and her staff.* FAO PHOTO

76   *American 4-H Club members leave for Europe.* U.S. DEPARTMENT OF
     AGRICULTURE PHOTO

77   *A Swedish forestry student.* UN PHOTO

83   *Thailand fishermen.* FAO PHOTO

83   *Chinese farm children.* FAO PHOTO

83   *Farm boys in Asia's rice fields.* FAO PHOTO

92   *A TB campaign plane carrying medical supplies.* UNICEF PHOTO

92   *A young convalescent TB patient in an Italian hospital.* UNICEF PHOTO

92   *Polish children wait for their BCG vaccination.* UNICEF PHOTO

93   *A doctor examines a Lapland baby.* UNICEF PHOTO

99   *Ecuador earthquake relief.* UNICEF PHOTO

99   *Bulgarian schoolgirls relish jam from Uruguay.* UNICEF PHOTO

99   *An anti-malaria team in India.* WHO PHOTO

108 *A UNESCO-sponsored school in Palestine.* AMERICAN FRIENDS SERVICE
     COMMITTEE PHOTO

108 *A makeshift school in Greece.* UNESCO PHOTO

108 *An outdoor school in Hungary.* UNESCO PHOTO

109 *A Polish girl's improvised science equipment.* UNESCO PHOTO

113 *Gymnastics in front of a bombed-out Greek school.* UNESCO PHOTO

113 *Yugoslav teen-agers build a railroad.* UNESCO PHOTO

121 *A United States gift box arrives in a French school.* AMERICAN JUNIOR
     RED CROSS PHOTO

121 *A United States gift box arrives in the Philippines.* AMERICAN JUNIOR
     RED CROSS PHOTO

121 *Washington, D.C., students pack a box for the Philippines.* AMERICAN JUNIOR RED CROSS PHOTO

125 *Vienna Week in a Los Angeles Junior High School.* LOS ANGELES BOARD OF EDUCATION PHOTO

125 *A Junior Red Cross exchange album.* AMERICAN JUNIOR RED CROSS PHOTO

125 *Students in the Los Angeles-adopted Vienna School.* BUNDESREAL-GYMNASIUM XVI, VIENNA, AUSTRIA PHOTO

130 *Pestalozzi Village, Trogen, Switzerland.* UNESCO PHOTO

130 *Boys in the Silvi Marina, Italy, Boys Town.* UNICEF PHOTO

130 *Fun at International Holiday Camp, Moulin Vieux, France.* UNESCO PHOTO

131 *The mayor of Children's Village, Dobbs Ferry, at Pestalozzi Village.* CHILDREN'S VILLAGE, DOBBS FERRY, N.Y., PHOTO

137 *International Work Campers, Ludwigshafen, Germany.* AMERICAN FRIENDS SERVICE COMMITTEE PHOTO

137 *College Work Campers, Grins, Austria.* AMERICAN FRIENDS SERVICE COMMITTEE PHOTO

137 *A Finnish Work Camper piles brush.* AMERICAN FRIENDS SERVICE COMMITTEE PHOTO

137 *Work Campers at Jamaica's Boys Town.* AMERICAN FRIENDS SERVICE COMMITTEE PHOTO

143 *A game at Pestalozzi Village.* UNESCO PHOTO

144 *Canadian high school students at Lake Success.* UN PHOTO

144 *Typical United States high school group discuss the UN.* LOS ANGELES BOARD OF EDUCATION PHOTO

145 *Bene Abbès, Algeria, start of a UNESCO expedition.* PIX, INC., PHOTO

151 *Science editor, Ritchie Calder, with English boys.* LONDON NEWS-CHRONICLE PHOTO

151 *Hungarian teen-agers improvise science equipment.* UNESCO PHOTO

156 *Desert farmer with primitive plow.* PIX, INC., PHOTO

157 *Boy in the International Youth Library, Munich.* INTERNATIONAL YOUTH LIBRARY, MUNICH, PHOTO

161 *A Mount Holyoke College girl gets ready for a French play.* UNESCO PHOTO

161 *A Dutch UNESCO library fellow in the Cleveland Public Library.* CLEVELAND, OHIO, PUBLIC LIBRARY PHOTO

161 *Camp Fire Girls bring a treasure chest to the St. Paul library.* ST. PAUL, MINNESOTA, PUBLIC LIBRARY PHOTO

169 *A girl of the Marbial Valley, Haiti.* UNESCO PHOTO

169 *A straw-thatched shack, Marbial Valley.* UNESCO PHOTO

169 *A model home, built by a UN team, Marbial Valley.* UNESCO PHOTO

169 *Home handcraft, Marbial Valley.* UNESCO PHOTO

175 *Food distribution center, Jogjakarta, Indonesia.* UNICEF PHOTO

175 *Jogjakarta boy helpers at the center.* UNICEF PHOTO

175 *Jogjakarta girl helpers at the center.* UNICEF PHOTO

175 *Delivering Jogjakarta supplies with a native conveyance.* UNICEF PHOTO

176 *A native doctor of Ceylon with young patients.* UNICEF PHOTO

177 *A twig toothbrush drill, Malnad, India.* WHO PHOTO

177 *A Greek doctor and patients, Terai, India.* UNICEF PHOTO

177 *A girl helps a baby nurse, Delhi, India.* WHO PHOTO

178 *Small feet need help for their upward climb.* UNICEF PHOTO

178 *A war-orphaned boy, always afraid.* UNICEF PHOTO

178 *A Greek girl and her makeshift home.* UNICEF PHOTO

179 *Eleanor Roosevelt reading a Spanish translation of the Declaration of Human Rights.* UN PHOTO

183 *Guatemala girls at milk time.* UNICEF PHOTO

14 • PARTNERS

183 *An Italian law student teaching village boys.* UNESCO PHOTO

188 *It was a happy washday when UNICEF soap arrived.* UNICEF PHOTO

189 *A small patient at Children's Hospital, Madras, India.* UNICEF PHOTO

191 *UNESCO's pilot project in Marbial Valley, Haiti.* UN PHOTO

192 *A little Arab girl waits for food in Israel.* UNICEF PHOTO

193 *Los Angeles pupils study UN organization.* LOS ANGELES BOARD OF EDUCATION PHOTO

199 *Yemenite children at Ein Shemer refugee camp.* UNICEF PHOTO

200 *UNICEF supplies go by pack train in the mountains.* UNICEF PHOTO

201 *Students keep informed on UN and UNESCO.* LOS ANGELES BOARD OF EDUCATION PHOTO

207 *Guatemala Indians transport UNICEF supplies to a remote village.* UNICEF PHOTO

MALAYAN SCHOOL
CHILDREN IN KAMPONG BAGAN BLAT GATHER FOR THEIR MID-MORNING MILK

PARTNERS
The United Nations and Youth

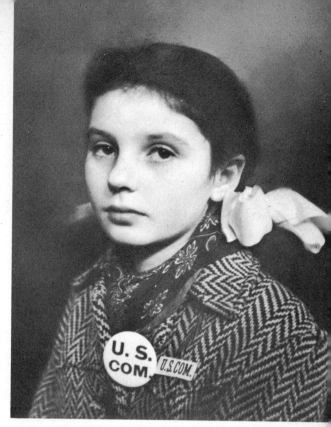

ON HER

WAY TO HER NEW AMERICAN HOME

A PLEDGE TO YOUTH Young people are
important in the United Nations. When fifty countries signed the United
Nations Charter on June 26, 1945, in San Francisco, they made their pledge
to youth in the first seventeen words of the Preamble: "We the peoples
of the United Nations, determined to save succeeding generations from the
Scourge of War . . ."

In the years ahead, building a better world for youth would be part of
all that the UN did. United Nations teams would travel far and wide, working with the many governments so that young people and children might
have more food, better health, more schools, more fun. Teen-agers everywhere would become United Nations partners in their own countries. They
would go out to young people of other nationalities, in meetings made possible by the United Nations, there learning to like and to understand their
new friends.

But first the delegates in San Francisco that June day knew that another
task for youth, a special task which was very great, lay before the United
Nations. In the countries left devastated by World War II were millions of

young people and children who needed food, clothes, medical care, and shelter. Driven from their homes by the fighting, many were still wandering about, living in caves, in the ruins of wrecked buildings, in burned-out railroad cars, any place where they could sleep or find shelter from the rain or the snow. Many were lost, not knowing where their parents were or even who they were. Others with their families were fortunate only in being together.

The United Nations, itself young, acted to help meet this great need.

Where was Hana Spotiva?

Blue-eyed Hana, with her yellow hair and fair complexion, who was only three years old the day in June 1942, when, at five o'clock in the morning, huge trucks rolled into the village of Lidice in Czechoslovakia. Jumping from the trucks, the Nazis woke up Hana and her mother and father, and ordered them outdoors with the others who lived in the village. Then they killed her father with the rest of the Lidice men and the boys over fifteen, and pushed her mother into a truck bound for a concentration camp.

They put Hana into one of the trucks loaded with the ninety-some other children. As they rolled away, behind them all Lidice was in flames. What the Nazis had done that day, they said, was because their official, SS General Heydrich, had been assassinated in Czechoslovakia. And they declared that Lidice would be an example to the people of the invaded countries of what they could expect if they defied their conquerors. It became, instead, a symbol to the civilized world of something that must never happen again.

Where did the Nazis take Hana?

Five years passed. The war was over. In an old flour mill in Esslingen, Germany, a group of men and women were searching among the vast number of records collected there. They were members of the Child Search staff of the International Tracing Service of the United Nations, and they were looking for Hana's name. Word had reached them that Hana's mother, still living despite her concentration camp imprisonment, wanted them to bring back her little girl.

The searchers found Hana's picture in the big scrapbook the Czech Government had made of all the Czech children kidnaped by the Nazis. What a pretty child, they thought. Would she have changed so that no one would be able to recognize her, now that she was eight years old? Changed, that is, if she were alive?

Then they took Hana's special card from one of the files. On it was the record of what a search team had learned about her when they had looked for all the Lidice children immediately after the end of the war. From Lidice, it seemed, the trucks loaded with the children had gone to Prague, from there to Lodz in Poland. In a camp in Lodz the children had all been examined for what their captors called racial desirability. Those considered best were then sent to one of the Nazi Lebensborn Homes — Lebensborn meaning "Fountain of Life." In these homes the chosen ones were given training in becoming "good Nazis," and later adopted into the families of high Nazi officials. Forged birth certificates were made out for the foster parents. And every Lebensborn boy or girl was insured.

Hana's card told what the first searchers had done. From two nurses who had worked in one of the Lebensborn homes they learned that the Lidice children had been taken to Lodz. On the Lodz records they found Hana's name with eleven others who had been chosen for the Fountain of Life. The insurance papers later confirmed this. Only twelve Lidice children of more than ninety had passed the Nazi tests. Of the others there was no trace.

That was what was on Hana's card five years later. She had been chosen. Her eyes were the right shade of blue. Her hair, the right yellow. She was well and strong, her mind alert. Although the first searchers then followed clue after clue, they had come in the end to a blank wall concerning her whereabouts. Somewhere, they felt sure, her adoption papers were on file. Somewhere, they found themselves believing, Hana was alive. But where?

Some time after those at Esslingen heard from Hana's mother, the Czech Ministry of Welfare received a long telegram from a man who signed himself a member of the denazification court in Frankfort. There was an adopted child in the village where he was now working, he said, who might be a Czech. At once the Czech Ministry relayed the message to Esslingen. In a matter of hours members of a search team were on their way in a jeep to the village the man had mentioned. When they arrived, it was only to find the telegram's information incorrect. There was no adopted child in that village, nor was the man himself there.

They did not give up. Following the clue of the man's being attached to the Frankfort court, they went to Frankfort. Another disappointment. The man's name was not on the court's list.

They did not give up. In all possible ways, through the newspapers, going to groups of people in Frankfort, talking with everyone they met, the searchers kept looking for the man who had sent the telegram. At last one of the team found a girl who said she knew him. He was in a village eighty kilometers away. Into the jeep again, and to that village. Again disappointment. The man was not there.

But wait. The local court worker told them that the widow of a Nazi official, who lived in the village, had a little adopted girl who must be about eight years of age. He would get out the adoption record.

Eagerly the searchers looked at the papers he brought them. There it was, Hana Spotiva. On the official adoption sheet her name had been changed to Hana Spot. But attached was a card on which her full name appeared. Hana was found.

The team did not go to Hana's Nazi home that day, however. Instead, with the evidence they now had, they returned to Frankfort to obtain from the Military Government an official permit for her removal and her return to her mother. Back again the next day with the permit, they drove to the widow's home. What would Hana say, they wondered, when they told her she was not a German child but a Czech? They had found some children who refused to believe such news, who had not wished to leave the only homes they could remember. Would Hana be one of them?

Brushing aside the widow's insistence that the child in her home was her own, the team members were firm that Hana must be brought to them. When the woman led Hana into the room, they knew beyond all doubt that here was Hana Spotiva of Lidice. For although she was five years older now, she clearly resembled the picture they had seen in the scrapbook at Esslingen. Kindly, understandingly, one of the team explained to her in German, the only language she knew, that this was not her real mother. Her real mother was waiting for them to bring Hana to her.

Hana stood silent, intent upon every word. When the searcher finished, Hana turned to the widow. "Pack up my things," she said. When the woman brought the bundle, she asked, "Are you sure they are all there?" Nothing more.

But as the jeep rushed along the road, she asked question after question about her mother. She tried to say, "I have come back to you, Mother," in Czech. Of the home she had left there was only, "Oh, I forgot my piggy bank." When one of her new friends told her that when they got to Prague they would give her a new bank for different money, she was satisfied.

Before they reached Prague, they stopped in Frankfort, where Hana stayed for a time in a camp run by the International Refugee Organization of the United Nations. To this camp other search teams were bringing all the Czech children whom they had thus far been able to find. When seventy-six Czech boys and girls were together there, the Military Government arranged for two special railroad coaches to take them to Prague, from which point they were to be returned to their parents, if they lived elsewhere in Czechoslovakia. Hana's mother was waiting for her at the Prague railway station. No one who saw that joyous welcome was ever to forget it.

The search team who found Hana, those who looked up the records about her in the Esslingen flour mill, were part of the International Refugee Organization of the United Nations. Establishing this organization was the United Nations' answer to the great need of the more than a million young people and children, men and women, who were still refugees in 1946.

At the time World War II ended in Europe in May 1945 there were more than eight million of these refugees, thousands upon thousands in the concentration camps where the Nazis had kept them prisoner, thousands upon thousands jamming the roads, thousands upon thousands everywhere, it seemed, in Germany and Hungary, the majority of whom wished to return to their homes as quickly as they could.

The Allied Armies of Occupation and hundreds of voluntary organizations, such as the Red Cross, went to their aid at once. Even though the UN Charter had not yet been signed, the nations already working together upon it formed the United Nations Relief and Rehabilitation Administration, UNRRA, to take charge until the UN itself could be set up.

Barracks that had belonged to the German Army, hotels, gymnasiums, and other public buildings were taken over, where the refugees were given shelter and food. All kinds of makeshift camps were erected. The quarters were not ideal, by any means. At first the only food that could be brought in for so many people was but little more than what would keep them alive. But it was food, and they had it every day. And shelter was shelter, of whatever kind.

Then began the UNRRA partners' staggering task of finding out how many of the eight million refugees wished to return to their old homes. About six and a half million did. Even though railroads were not yet rebuilt, although bridges were still out, although all too few trucks were in good running order, the homeward trek began, continuing steadily, until by the end of 1946 most of the six and a half million men and women, young people and children, had been returned.

Remaining were the more than a million who no longer wished to live where their homes had been before the war. It was of them that the United Nations took special thought as it faced the fact in San Francisco that UNRRA was scheduled to end shortly. Who now would do the work of finding new homes in all parts of the world for the refugees? Who would search for the men and women who had disappeared during the war? Who would look for the lost teen-agers and children? Who would see to it that the refugees were given food and other necessary things each day while they awaited word of where they were to go?

The United Nations' answer was to establish the International Refugee Organization. And the UN General Assembly made this important decision: Not one of the refugees, young or old, was to be forced to go where he or she did not wish to go. Within two years money contributed by eighteen countries through their governments was to support the work done by IRO.

William Hallam Tuck, an able American engineer and executive, was appointed IRO's Director-General. Joining the hundreds of men and women already at work among the Displaced Persons, as the refugees left behind were now called, came many more for IRO's staff. What that staff was to accomplish in the three years just ahead was truly remarkable. To give all the waiting DP's places to live, center after center was to be constructed until the number of them reached seven hundred. The supplies the staff brought in were to come from twenty-seven countries on five continents. The health sanitation experts, the doctors, the nurses were to do their work so well that there was no serious epidemic anywhere. As the staff worked to find new homes in distant countries for the DP's, they were to bring together one of the largest peacetime fleets ever assembled. As many

ONE OF THE SEVEN HUNDRED CENTERS
FOR IRO REFUGEES

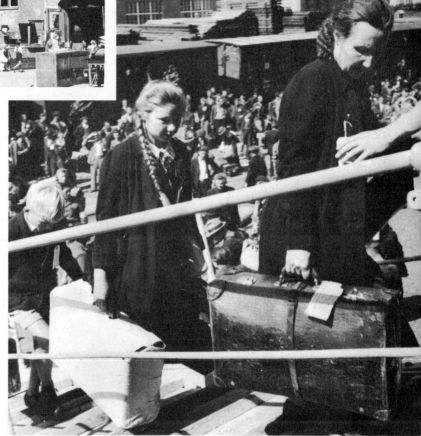

BOARDING AN IRO
CHARTERED SHIP
TO BEGIN
THEIR NEW LIFE

LATVIAN
DACE EPERMANIS,
150,000TH DP
TO ENTER
THE UNITED STATES,
AND HER FAMILY
ARE WARMLY
WELCOMED

as thirty-six of these ships were to be at sea at a single time, all filled with DP's on their way to their new homes. Schools for adults as well as for teen-agers and children were to be organized in the centers.

Through all their more than busy days, wrestling with difficulties too numerous to describe, IRO's staff, recruited from forty different countries, speaking nearly all the world's languages, was to work together in harmony and devotion, a United Nations team in action.

The DP's themselves did more than wait for the welcome word that there was some place in the world where they were wanted. By far the majority of them came forward to help those who were helping them. Under their IRO administrators they organized in town groups, with DP mayors, policemen, and other officials. DP doctors made their rounds and worked in the hospitals that were set up. DP carpenters helped erect needed buildings. DP cooks worked in kitchens. DP dressmakers made clothes. DP shoemakers were busy.

And DP teachers volunteered for the schools. At first these schools were necessarily very crude, often without books or other equipment. Many a teacher stayed up late at night writing down from memory lessons in history or arithmetic so that his pupils would have something from which to study the next day. It was not long, however, before classes in languages, geography, and the other usual school subjects were well organized, and vocational training was being given as well, in upward of twelve trades, including automobile mechanics, radio, masonry, farming, cooking, dressmaking, and the like. The classes for adults were similar in their variety. It was a great public school system, whose teachers came from many countries, whose students were more eager to learn, it seemed, than any had ever been before.

A record card was kept for each DP. On it was written all that would help in finding the right kind of future home for him or for her. If a girl had musical talent and liked to play the piano or other instrument, that was put down. If a boy was skillful in mechanics, note of that was made. If a teen-ager had some special ambition for his or her future career, that, too, was recorded. To be sure, these ambitions might not last, but for the present they were important to each young person's happiness.

For the nearly four thousand lost teen-agers and children, those whom the workers called "unaccompanied," special centers were set up. Often the children brought in to these centers found it difficult to realize that they were among friends. Life had treated them so cruelly, they could not now believe in kindness.

In one center, where the newcomers were a group of boys and girls aged ten and eleven, all were unusually suspicious and resentful. The figures tattooed on their arms told the story. They had been young concentration camp prisoners, numbers only to their captors.

One of the IRO workers talked with their young leader. "This place is different," she told him. "Here you are free to play as you wish, to have fun."

The leader went back to his companions for a conference, returning in a few minutes with a question. "Did you mean it when you said we could play as we wish?"

The worker nodded. "Certainly, so long as you do not hurt each other."

In seconds bedlam broke loose. The children shouted, yelled, screamed, ran around like mad. Even when they kept it up the following day, the IRO workers made no move to stop them. When, at last, they quieted down, they knew beyond all doubt that this place *was* different, that they were indeed among friends.

In the British Zone in Germany sixty teen-agers had their own Teen Town, running it by self-government with their elected officers. They did much of the necessary work. They ran their own sports, dramatics, glee club, and orchestra. For their home economics, the girls attended a school in the nearby town of Verden, the boys a trade school there.

In all the camps and centers teen-agers were as busy as the Teen Town citizens. They took care of younger children. They helped in the kitchens, the hospitals. They were assistants in everything, in fact, that youth can do. And they organized their own club groups.

International youth organizations of many kinds sent men and women to the centers to help them, such as the Y.M.C.A. and the Y.W.C.A., the Girl Scouts, the Boy Scouts. What the Boy Scouts International Bureau did was typical of the way in which all worked. Everywhere in the DP centers were boys who had been Boy Scouts back home, Czechoslovakian, Estonian, Hungarian, Yugoslavian, Ukrainian Boy Scouts, as well as those from other countries. Even before the Bureau arrived, they had gotten together for troop meetings, and DP Scoutmasters had volunteered to help them.

Then J. R. Monnet, a Scouter of long experience, arrived on the scene from the Bureau to help the troops already under way and to organize new ones. Under his direction courses for new Scoutmasters were started. And it was not long before many thousand DP Boy Scouts were holding patrol meetings, working on proficiency badges, going on week-end hikes. They had their own summer camps, too, with swimming, woodcraft hours, camp-fire evenings, and the other activities that Boy Scouts around the world enjoy.

Wherever the teen-agers were, there were always some who showed themselves to have the same kind of searching ability as those of the Esslingen teams. One of these was a thirteen-year-old Polish girl in an IRO camp near Heidelberg, whom the workers called "the fierce, silent one." One day she disappeared, returning some time later with an old woman who was her great-aunt. She would not say where she had been nor how she had found her aunt, nor would the old woman reveal it. But there the aunt was. This was only the start. Again and again the fierce, silent one went off, some-times coming back alone, other times with yet another member of her family, until seven of them were together.

The headquarters of the search for all who were lost was at Arolsen, Germany — the International Tracing Service. There, in mammoth files, were index cards with all the information that could be found about the more than six million people who were reported missing. The Child Search Bureau in Esslingen was that part of the International Tracing Service whose work was to look for lost youth.

No detective in any story ever followed clues with greater ingenuity than the Child Search workers. In one center they picked up a certain small girl, wandering around alone, who could not tell them her name nor where she had lived. On the chance that someone in her family might recognize her, the workers decided to send her picture to all the newspapers pub-lished in nearby towns. Sure enough, a letter shortly arrived from a rope-worker. "My wife and I think that little girl looks as our lost Drusi would by now."

A ropemaker — had the child watched her father at his work? If she were now to see someone busy with the same thing, would she remember, perhaps? It was worth trying. One of the workers then sought out a neigh-bor ropemaker, who gave her lessons. Not long afterward she sat down with her materials near the children at their play. The children stopped their game and ran toward her to see what she was doing.

But the little unknown one ran most swiftly of them all. "My daddy can do that, too!" she shouted. It was Drusi.

It was in Switzerland that the workers found Adolf Rashid J——, in a village to which a group of French children had fled. His shoes were worn through. His clothes were ragged. There were no papers of any kind in his pockets. Only the tag tied around his neck with string told them anything at all about him. "Adolf Rashid J——," it said, with the date of his birth.

The children with him knew who they were and where they had lived in France. But none of them could remember where Adolf had joined them. "He just came along," they said. Adolf himself could tell nothing about his parents or his home.

It occurred to the workers that since Rashid was such an unusual name, he might have been called after some town or village in Europe where he was born. But when they got out the atlases and directories, no Rashid could they find.

One day when the children began talking about boats, Adolf boasted, "My mother and father and I were on a boat."

Was it a clue at last? Just possibly, for when a baby is born on a boat, his parents often give him that boat's name. Checking marine records, the searchers found that a British vessel called *Rashid* had plied the Mediterranean before the war. With the help of the British Consulate in Switzerland, the log of the *Rashid* for the date of Adolf's birth was examined. He was there. There, too, were the names of his parents.

When they told Adolf, he was happier than he had been for a long time. No longer was he different from the other children. He, too, now belonged somewhere. Having been born on a British ship, he was a British boy, for that is the British law. Today Adolf, whose parents have never been found, has a home in England.

While the search teams were following their clues, hundreds of IRO workers were busy with another kind of search, that for homes in all parts of the world to which the waiting DP's could go. First IRO sent word to the various governments about the many kinds of workers among the DP's, the teachers, the plumbers, the doctors, carpenters, engineers, farmers, artists, foresters, writers, textile experts, domestic workers, and on and on down a long list.

And the governments sent back their invitations for the DP's to come
to them. Some of these invitations were for individual workers. Others
were for families. Still others were for large groups who would live and
work together in their new homes. Australia, Canada, and Great Britain
were the first to invite these groups, but the idea spread, and other such
invitations followed. Belgium welcomed twenty thousand miners, and in
three months their families joined them. In the highlands of Brazil, at
Goias, today over two hundred DP families are living together. Each family
has its own house with enough land around it for a garden and a barn for
cattle. Outside the village are the fields that all plant and cultivate together.

What of invitations to the DP teen-agers? At first it looked as though
people preferred small children in their homes, for many more wished to
adopt them than those who were older. IRO set to work to change this
situation. J. Donald Kingsley, the experienced and dynamic American executive who had succeeded Mr. Tuck as Director-General of IRO, sent out
special word about the fine teen-age young people among the DP's. He
told how splendidly they were doing their share in the camps and centers,
what fine Boy Scouts and other organization members they had proved
themselves to be. So many invitations then arrived for the teen-agers that
in the end they were in greater demand proportionately than any other
group. Australia invited five hundred of them to come to homes there. The
United States, Sweden, and New Zealand followed suit. Other countries
joined in.

As with all DP's, just which invitation should be accepted for any
teen-ager was carefully considered by the IRO workers both at the centers
and in the country extending the invitation. Each boy's, each girl's record
card was studied so that the home chosen would be one in which each
would be happy and well cared for. The foster parents, too, were taken
into careful consideration, so that they would be happy, as well, in the
choice made. When the decision was made to accept the invitation, each
young person was given a final physical checkup, for it was an IRO rule
that only those who were in good physical condition could leave.

Then the teen-agers who had been chosen went to IRO's embarkation
centers, where each joined a group made up of others bound for the same
country. While IRO workers made out the necessary legal papers and
arranged for transportation, the young people attended classes in which

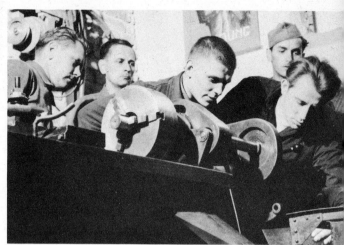

DP GIRLS LEARNED SEWING AND
DP BOYS LEARNED TOOLMAKING

SINGING TIME IN AN IRO BOYS'
AND GIRLS' CAMP NEAR
NUREMBERG, GERMANY

"TELL US ANOTHER STORY, PLEASE"
— AND THE IRO WORKER OBLIGES

they were told what life would be like in their new homes. And they were given special instruction in the language they would speak there.

They were very grateful for this special farewell help. When one group of nine teen-age boys left for the United States, all signed a joint letter to their IRO friend whose special embarkation charge they had been. "You will understand that we are impatient to set out for our journey," they wrote, "that we are full of happiness to be shipped tomorrow. But we are quite aware that all this is possible only with your assistance and help. How shall we thank you? How shall we show our gratitude?

"As the sign of our gratitude, please accept this as our earnest promise: Always to try to do our best in our new country. Always to try to become good citizens. Always to try to become good Americans."

In the United States, the task of finding new homes for the DP teen-agers and children, welcoming them when they arrive, and seeing that they are taken to their foster homes has been carried on by the Committee for the Care of European Children. Working together on this Committee are men and women from Catholic, Jewish, and Protestant organizations. Through them every arriving teen-ager, every child, has had a special welcome at the pier where his ship has docked or at the airfield where his plane has landed. The Committee's workers have carried on the Reception Center in the Bronx in New York City, where the young people and children first stay in attractive surroundings for three weeks or so, where they are made to feel at home among new friends and become accustomed to life in a new country. There is gaiety at the Center. In the singing and the games shyness vanishes. And when these new young Americans have to leave, they say good-by with happy confidence in what lies ahead.

The workers at the Center remember affectionately the many young people and children who have been with them. There was small Freddie, so full of importance when he arrived. He had treasures! Gathering together a suitable audience of the other children, triumphantly he produced his first treasure — a cake of soap. Satisfied with their exclamations of respect, he pulled out his second treasure — a cake of soap. The respect changed to awe. Whereupon Freddie revealed his third — a cake of soap. Beyond all doubt Freddie was a Very Important Person.

That was all for the time being, but when one of his new older friends took Freddie up to bed, he beckoned to her secretively. Opening his dresser drawer, he pointed to — a cake of soap. Looking down at Freddie's animated little face, the worker knew why he and the other children were so excited over soap. It wasn't that they had had none 'of it in their IRO centers. There was plenty of soap there. No, it was because of a memory, soon to be buried deep, she hoped, of days and nights of anxious flight when life itself was almost their only possession.

Freddie was on his way to the home of an American music professor and his wife. When he arrived, his soap was promptly relegated to second place. For there in the living room stood a grand piano. To the delight of his new parents, today Freddie likes nothing quite so much as listening to "my own father" play. Together he and his father and mother sing the Latvian songs that Freddie still remembers.

For the teen-agers who have come to the Center the U.S. Committee also has great admiration. They are such ambitious young people. That is, most of them are. Some, as is understandable, are still resentful about what happened to them during the war. But many more are looking forward, not back.

"When I was a little girl, I wanted to be a doctor because I thought a doctor knew very much," fourteen-year-old Regina wrote for the Center's mimeographed newspaper, *New Life,* in her recently acquired English. "The doctor in her white dress looked very nice. Therefore I wanted to be a doctor, too.

"In our camp in Germany I helped in the little hospital where babies were being taken care of. I saw how our doctor worked and I liked to look at her work, and I thought that when I could be a doctor, I could do as she did. So now I think about my future, and I still want to be a doctor. I know that when people are sick, they are unhappy. They cannot work and then they have no money for their food and clothes and other things which they need every day. The doctor can help the most."

Regina's American parents have told her that if, after she has finished high school, she still wishes to be a doctor, she may go on to college and medical school.

George from Belgium, in his late teens when he arrived in the United States, was eager to go to college. His American parents arranged for him to do so, and were proud when George was graduated with honors. By that time George had decided to become a teacher in the field of languages.

Today he is back at his college, studying for his master's degree and earning his way by teaching in the language department.

Imre from Hungary said he wanted to be a farmer, and the Committee found a home for him on an Iowa farm where after school and during vacations he helps his foster father. He still says he wishes to be a farmer, and after high school the plan is for him to go to an agricultural school. In his classes at the DP center Esyergalyos of Latvia showed special talent for mechanics. His home, too, is in Iowa, where his Saturday job is in a local garage.

For some of the teen-agers special plans must be made. Now and then they are afraid of going to live in private homes with families. Having been in a center for so long, they prefer that kind of life. Musical Annika was one of these. For her the Committee found a place in an American Protestant home for young people, where she is happy in having a piano to play and a music teacher.

Some teen-agers, like Jack, wish to go right to work. Jack had a definite plan — he wished to be an American chef. So his New England foster parents found an opening for him in a large Boston hotel, where he started as a kitchen runner. He did so well as a runner that soon he was given a promotion, then another, and another, until he was eligible for the hotel's Junior Epicurean course. Jack is on his way.

It has not always been easy for the DP teen-agers to become used to new ways in the countries to which they have gone. It has not always been easy for their foster parents, either. But wherever there has been a real wish on both sides to understand each other, more often than not that understanding has come about.

So it was that month by month the number of DP's left behind became smaller. So it was that one by one many of the centers were closed down. But all too many refugees still remained, the "Hard Core," those to whom no invitations had come.

Tragically some of the Hard Core were men and women with splendid educations, trained specialists of unusual ability. They had been passed over by the various countries for those who do manual labor. Others were old or blind or crippled. There were families to whom homes were refused because one of their children had lost a leg or an arm in the war. Governments were reluctant to assume responsibility for such handicapped youth lest later they be unable to support themselves and so become public charges.

Mr. Kingsley sent out special appeals for all the Hard Core. And again the peoples of the world responded. One by one some of the specialists did receive invitations at last. Some of the handicapped, too, were welcomed. Norway offered to take a large group of the totally blind, with IRO helping by providing the money to build a new wing on one of the Norwegian Homes for the Blind. Belgium invited a number of the aged to come and spend the rest of their lives in one of her homes. Other plans were worked out by other governments.

And the kind nuns of the Immaculate Conception Home in Lodi, New Jersey, through the American Catholic Committee for Refugees, invited small, one-legged Polish Frankie and his seven brothers and sisters to come to them in the United States. It was a gallant, not-so-little family that arrived. All through their concentration camp years, with their parents lost and no trace of them ever found, Frankie's teen-age brothers and sisters had kept the family together. Because the older ones had been made Nazi slave laborers, they had been given more food to keep up their strength for working. But they had not kept that food for themselves. They had shared everything.

From the first Frankie was a delight to everyone at the home in Lodi. He was so gay, so merry, so eager. Not long after a visitor saw him hopping about on his crutch in a baseball game, an artificial leg arrived for Frankie.

"Now I can roller-skate," he gleefully announced.

Roller-skate he did, becoming so expert that the neighbors up and down the street were soon boasting about him. A doctor, seeing him speed past, invited him to come and skate for the patients in a veterans' hospital near by, where GI's who had lost an arm or a leg were convalescing. The doctor felt sure that seeing Frankie would encourage them.

It did. More than one GI declared, "Well, if a kid can do that, I can, too." From veterans' hospital to veterans' hospital Frankie went then, until all were agreed that no one in the state of New Jersey had helped crippled GI's more than he. Handicapped? Not Frankie!

As the time approached in 1950 for IRO to end its work, according to UN plan, Mr. Kingsley and his staff redoubled their efforts for the some twenty-five thousand DP's still left behind. The records of the International Tracing Service were transferred to the High Commissioners for Germany, so that any clues discovered in the future could be used in connection with those cards still stamped "Not found."

Hopeless though the situation may seem for ever tracing these still missing men and women, young people and children, now and then word does come from some distant spot in the world which is the beginning of reuniting families once more. Such was the word that came to Maruja, in her foster home in Missouri. She was only eleven when, with a number of other Spanish children, she fled from the fighting. Rescued from the water-logged old barge on which they were drifting in the Atlantic Ocean, they were brought to the United States. Maruja was sent to Missouri, where she attended school and enjoyed the clubs and other activities. When she entered high school, she was elected captain of the cheer leaders.

Much as she loved her foster parents and her new friends, she never lost her hope and her dream that someday her mother and father would be found. Month after month passed, until she was in the sixth year of her stay. Then came the day when the longed-for letter arrived from IRO's Tracing Service. Her mother and father were alive, in England. How soon could Maruja join them? Very soon!

When one thinks of the time and thought and work that went into helping Hana, Imre, Annika, Jack, Frankie, and Maruja, only six young people, the record of all that IRO did in three years takes on new meaning. By 1950 IRO helped in some way more than one million, four hundred and ninety-nine thousand refugees. It found new homes for more than seven hundred and ninety thousand, three hundred and ninety-eight DP's. The International Tracing Service successfully traced seventy thousand, two hundred and fifty-three missing people, of whom two thousand, nine hundred and seventy-five were lost young people and children located by the Child Search Teams.

BY SHIP, BY PLANE,
YOUTH'S NEEDS WERE ANSWERED

FOR THÉRÈSE, PIERRE, AND THE OTHERS

When they found her, there in the dark, damp cellar of a bombed-out French farmhouse, with rubble and refuse on every side, they thought she was ten or eleven. Later, they discovered she was fourteen. But she was so small, so thin, it was no wonder they guessed her younger than she was.

Jeanine, for that was the name they gave her, not knowing any other, did not welcome those who came to take her to the nearby town where in a building that had escaped the bombing kindly townspeople had set up a center where young French refugees were being cared for. She screamed and clawed and struggled, and it was with the greatest difficulty that they got her into the car.

At the center, even after they had taken off her rags, had given her a bath, clothes, and warm soup, she was not grateful. And because stealing had for so long been the only way in which she could get anything to eat, she snatched food even from the small children, fighting back fiercely when they defended their share.

That she had lived in their part of France, those at the center could tell from the way she spoke. But she would not answer their questions about where her home had been, how she had gotten to the bombed-out farmhouse. Some of the workers thought this was because she was still suspicious, even though she gradually grew more manageable. Others felt she did not remember what had happened to her during those terrible years of war, and wasn't that understandable? Such things are best forgotten.

The doctor, who examined her at the small clinic in the corner of a church and who gave her cod-liver oil, said not to bother her with any more questions. The food she was now getting was already bringing back her strength. Soon she would remember, he thought.

One day, with the truck that delivered food supplies to the center, a visitor arrived to talk with the workers, asking questions of them and jotting down their replies in a notebook. Later, she sang songs with them. One of the songs was an old French ballad. Jeanine did not join in, but when the lovely melody filled the room, she leaned forward, clenching her hands and frowning intently. Just as they were finishing the first verse, she jumped up, and running across the room to the worker standing in the doorway, threw her arms around her and cried out the name of a village more than fifty miles away. Jeanine had remembered at last.

Eagerly, then, the workers listened to all that she so feverishly poured forth. She was Thérèse. At home there had been Maman, Papa, an older brother, Pierre. Although she still did not mention a family name, to have Thérèse, Pierre, and the name of the village was enough. Next day, in the dilapidated old car belonging to the center, one of the workers set out with Thérèse.

As they approached the village, Thérèse was beside herself with excitement. What happened next was — so the worker later told the others at the center — a veritable miracle. When they stopped on the village street, a lame man came out of a small shop near by. Like a flash Thérèse leaped from the car.

"My uncle!" she cried. "My uncle Jacques!"

"My little Thérèse," the man sobbed. And the pale, barefooted boy who followed the man threw his arms around them both.

The story the man told was a sad one, all too familiar in war-torn France. Thérèse's father had gone off to the war and had not returned. Her mother had been shot by the Nazis for refusing to give up their cow. The enemy had taken Pierre away with them. Thérèse, the little Thérèse, had run off into the woods, and no one from the village had been able to come upon even a trace of her. He himself, coming back wounded from the fighting, had found only his wife, Georgette, awaiting him. His brother's family were gone, all gone.

After a while Pierre had returned from Germany, where the Nazis had taken him and where they had forced him to work long hours in a factory. When the war was over, he had wandered off by himself, hoping to find his way home. To him, then, had come a man who took him to a camp where many other war refugees were being looked after. As soon as they could, the camp people had arranged for his transportation back home, and here he was. Now also the little Thérèse had come. Praise to the good God, she, too, was home.

That home, a mile or so outside the village, was a small farm where the three of them had been managing to stay alive. It was not easy. The enemy had taken all his good tools, all the pots and pans from his Georgette's kitchen. Their own cow had long since died. The few seeds he had planted last spring had grown so poorly there had been little use in trying to do anything with them. And then the drought had come. Yes, life was hard. But they still had their farm and there they would now care for Thérèse.

After the happy moments of Aunt Georgette's surprised, overwhelming joy, the worker asked about the young people and the children of the village and on the other farms near by. Did they have enough food? Sadly Jacques and Georgette shook their heads. No one had enough food even now, and winter was coming.

When the worker bade them good-by, she said, "I shall come back. I shall come back soon with good news."

She kept her promise. The following week, this time with a man on the staff of the national government of France, she returned. But before going out to Jacques's and Georgette's farm, they stopped for a long talk with the mayor of the village.

Then to Thérèse, to Pierre, to Jacques, and to Georgette they took the glad word. "Soon there will be food. For the babies, the small children, even for those as old as Pierre. Good milk and bread, strength-giving meat and vegetables. Lift up your hearts. The food will come."

The welcome word the worker brought to Jacques, Georgette, Pierre, and Thérèse that day was the same that hundreds of thousands of young people and children in the war-devastated countries of Europe were hearing. It was the word that within three years was to come to millions of others, in other parts of the world as well. Word followed by the food itself and clothing and medicine, brought to them by the United Nations International Children's Emergency Fund in partnership with each girl's, each boy's own government.

It was at a meeting of the General Assembly of the United Nations on December 11, 1946, that Fiorello LaGuardia, then Director-General of the UN Economic and Social Council and Mayor of New York City, proposed that a United Nations International Children's Emergency Fund be established to help care for the young victims of World War II, a fund to which the governments of the world would be invited to contribute.

The proposal was unanimously adopted by the General Assembly in a resolution stating that as many as possible of these young people and children up to eighteen years of age were to receive help from the Fund "on the basis of need, without discrimination because of race, creed, nationality, or political belief."

In voting that such a fund be established, the General Assembly's delegates to the United Nations fully appreciated all that the many voluntary organizations were so gallantly doing. They knew of the valiant efforts being made by the war-devastated countries themselves for their youth. UNRRA, too, had helped. But all of them together had been able to make only a start.

Each of the delegates at the General Assembly that day quickly sent word to his country about the Fund. And from around the world came the answer: "We are glad to contribute our share," with the pledge of what each government would give. Large as the promised amount was, however — and it was millions of dollars — it was not enough, so great was the emergency, so many were the young people and children in desperate need of help.

At the suggestion of Mr. Aake Ording of Norway, therefore, the General Assembly voted to establish the United Nations Appeal for Children, to which every individual citizen anywhere, young and old, might contribute. Again the generous answer came back, from men, women, young

MILLIONS HEARD THE GLAD WORD, "FOOD HAS COM

people, even from children, in all parts of the world, and from all kinds of organizations and schools and churches. Contributions small as well as large, including shillings and pence from those in the South Sea Islands.

"Sing-aut sorri," the letter began which went out through the Solomons, New Guinea, Papua, and the other islands, telling about the appeal. "Sing-aut sorri," which is pidgin English for "Sing-out sorry" and is the South Sea Islanders' call for help.

Within three years the peoples of fifty countries were to contribute through their governments to the Fund and with their own contributions to the appeal. The peoples of Australia, Austria, Belgium, Bulgaria. Of Canada, Ceylon, Chile, Costa Rica, Cuba, Czechoslovakia. Of Denmark, the Dominican Republic, Ecuador, Finland, France, Greece, Guatemala. Of Honduras, Hungary, Iceland, India, Israel, Italy. Of Liberia, Lichtenstein, Luxembourg, Monaco, Mozambique. Of the Netherlands, Newfoundland, New Zealand, Nicaragua, Norway. Of Pakistan, Panama, Peru, the Philippines, Poland, San Marino, Sweden, Switzerland, Thailand, the Union of South Africa. Of the United Kingdom of Great Britain and northern Ireland, the British Colonial Territories. Of the United States of America, the United States of Indonesia, Uruguay, Venezuela, Yugoslavia. In this stirring list are some countries who were themselves very much in need of the help the Fund could bring their youth. Yet they joined with the others for the sake of the young people and children in whatever war-devastated country they were to be found.

The money was ready. Who was to direct its spending? Who would see to it that food, clothing, and medical care quickly reached the millions who were waiting?

The United Nations is large, with many parts. Its work extends around the world. Every day thousands of men and women are busy carrying out its projects. Each knows just what to do because the United Nations is carefully planned and organized. So, now, with UNICEF, as the Fund was already being called. It was given its special place in the great UN organization.

That place was in the Economic and Social Council, established by the UN Charter to help bring about better standards of living throughout the world. There UNICEF would work side by side with the Council's permanent Specialized Agencies, such as the Food and Agriculture Organization — FAO; the World Health Organization — WHO; and the UN Educational, Scientific, and Cultural Organization — UNESCO.

This sounds complicated. Actually, it is all very much like the clubs in your school. Your clubs are part of your school. The Specialized Agencies are part of the Economic and Social Council. Each of your clubs is organized for a certain purpose. Your Debating Club is for debating. Your Junior Red Cross is for Red Cross work, and so on. Each of the Specialized Agencies is organized for a definite purpose, as its name shows.

Whether or not you join a club is for you to decide. The nations of the world join one of the Specialized Agencies only if they wish to do so. If you wish to join more than one club, you may. Many nations belong to more than one Specialized Agency, some belong to them all. To carry on your club's work, you pay dues. The money to run each Specialized Agency comes from the amounts its member nations pay into the treasury each year.

Sometimes, in addition to what your clubs are doing in your school, a number of you wish to start a special project, such as raising money to help equip your new recreation field. To launch your project, you bring it up before your student body, perhaps at your assembly, where it is discussed and voted upon. If the vote is favorable, a special committee is appointed to carry out the project.

UNICEF, a special project of the Economic and Social Council, was established in this same way. When the Council voted in favor of having it, the plan was laid before the General Assembly for discussion and decision. When the Assembly voted favorably upon it, it was returned to the Council for carrying out.

UNICEF was told just what its work was to be, and wherein that work was different from IRO's. UNICEF was to work with the governments of the various war-devastated nations, helping each to meet the needs of its own children and young people who were still within its national boundaries. IRO's responsibility, on the other hand, was to take complete care of all the people, young and older, who were outside their own countries, either because they had fled from them during the fighting or because they had been taken away by the enemy. It was workers from UNICEF who came to Thérèse in the bombed-out farmhouse, and to Pierre, as well, there in his French home. When he was wandering about in Germany, it was the workers of IRO who cared for him.

To set up UNICEF's organization, the Economic and Social Council elected an executive board with twenty-six members from as many countries. To take charge of the Fund's work, Maurice Pate was chosen, an American businessman of wide and valuable experience who during World War I served with Herbert Hoover in American relief work and during World War II was in charge of the prisoners-of-war program of the International Red Cross.

At once Mr. Pate set to work choosing those who would work with him on UNICEF's staff. As soon as they accepted, they became members of the United Nations Secretariat, which is made up of all the men and women who have full-time paid positions with the United Nations.

Head of the Secretariat, the man responsible for seeing that all the work of the United Nations runs smoothly, is Trygve Lie, first UN Secretary-General. The UN Charter states that the Secretary-General is to be the chief administrative officer of the entire UN organization, that he is to act in that capacity at all meetings of the General Assembly, the Security Council, the Economic and Social Council, and the Trusteeship Council. Since the day in February 1946 when Trygve Lie was inducted into office, he has faithfully worked to carry this out.

UNICEF has always had a real friend in Trygve Lie. And an important one, for again and again he has broadcast to the peoples of the world the story of UNICEF's work among youth. And because the peoples everywhere respect and admire him, because they rely on his honesty, they have not failed to answer with new support for the Fund.

Trygve Lie was born in Oslo, Norway, on July 16, 1896. When his father, who was a carpenter, died while Trygve was still small, his mother ran a boarding house in Grorud, a suburb of Oslo, to support her son and herself. There Trygve went through high school, doing all kinds of odd jobs to add to the family income.

But no matter how busy he was, he always had time for sports. "I was practically born on skis," he says. Tall and strong, he was also good at wrestling, skating, and tennis. Whenever he appeared for a boating party in the fjords, there were shouts of welcome, for he was jolly, full of fun. What was more, his friends could count on his being good-humored no matter what happened. Later, when he was living in the United States, he was to add baseball to his sports enthusiasms.

Those who hired him liked him, too. He stuck to his jobs and did them well. When he was only fifteen, he was made executive secretary of the local health insurance company. When he was sixteen, he was elected president of a branch of the Labor Party. By that time young Trygve knew what interested him more than anything else — people. He liked all kinds. He wanted to help them. When, therefore, he decided to study law, he made up his mind to become a lawyer for workingmen and their families.

He held to that decision, earning his way through the Oslo University Law School by doing chores in the office of the Norwegian Labor Party. Upon his graduation, he was appointed Secretary-General of the Party.

He married his childhood sweetheart, and three daughters were born to them. As soon as each was old enough, she joined in the family skiing, skating, tennis, and boating trips. Mr. Lie likes having the house full of his daughters' friends, for he has a special place in his heart for youth.

When the Labor Party was elected to head Norway's national government, Trygve Lie was first appointed General Counsel, then Minister of Justice. As Minister of Justice, he had as an important part of his work the settling of labor disputes. During the years just before World War II there were almost no strikes in Norway, chiefly because, so people said, those on both sides sat down to talk things over with Mr. Lie. In some way or other, the majority of the differences were ironed out. He was admired by both employers and employees. And he was fair.

Mr. Lie's next position with the Norwegian Government was as Minister of Commerce. It was then, shortly after World War II began, that he sent out his famous radio message to Norway's great merchant fleet at sea. The Nazis had invaded Norway, and Norway had decided to fight. Although Mr. Lie and his staff were being driven from place to place, they were courageously organizing supplies for the parts of Norway not yet occupied.

When the Nazis demanded over the air that the fleet surrender, Trygve Lie countered with: "Do not surrender. Go into the ports of our Allies." Without exception, the captains of the Norwegian fleet obeyed.

Trygve Lie was one of the last of Norway's cabinet members to leave for London, where the work of the government was then carried on. When the war was over, it was as Foreign Minister that he went to the United Nations conference in San Francisco, to head the Norwegian delegation. One of his daughters accompanied him, as the delegation's secretary.

No one who knew Trygve Lie was surprised when he was chosen chief administrative officer for the United Nations, its Secretary-General. On the day of his induction into office he said to the member nations: "I am the servant of you all. . . . Certain of your support, I look to the future with confidence. . . . We may find difficulties and obstacles ahead of us. But the harder the task, the higher the prize. It is the future of the whole civilized world which is at stake."

In the records of the United Nations, no word more frequently appears than "team." The UNICEF team was ready. It had its special place in the United Nations. It had its Secretary-General. It had its executive board. It had its Director-General, its staff. It had the money for its work. What should the Fund do first with that money?

AT LAKE SUCCESS TRYGVE LIE EXTENDS A WELCOME
TO AN INTERNATIONAL EXCHANGE STUDENT FROM LUXEMBOURG

IT WAS A HAPPY DAY IN SKAFI,
MACEDONIA, WHEN BLANKETS CAME

THE SAME
IN EVERY LANGUAGE
Arturo hurried along the
road toward school. No dragging feet this time, no wishing he were anywhere but there. Today, when the other boys laughed at him, what he had
to tell would wipe those hateful grins from their faces. Today, when they
called his grandmother an old stupid, a know-nothing, they would swallow
their words!

The trouble he had been having since day before yesterday had seemed
even worse because everyone else at school was so happy. He, too, had
been happy at first. It had been wonderful, that was exactly the word for
it, to have the soup and the milk. Yet it had been the milk that caused his
trouble.

Perhaps his grandmother would have understood if the Old Teacher
had mentioned it the afternoon he brought the good news to them. Two
weeks ago, that was, after the stranger had driven up in a car. As soon
as his visitor left, the Old Teacher had gone from house to house. Food
would come, he said, not for one week only but for many weeks. Food for

all their young who had been hungry for so long. Food from kind, far-distant friends, who were partners with their own Italian Government. Food that the village women would take turns cooking and serving each school day.

No one had been surprised that it was the Old Teacher who had such good news. He it was who, when there was nobody to be schoolteacher after the war was over, had said of course they would have a school. Although he was old and became tired easily, he himself would teach it. What if the schoolhouse had been wrecked? Let the young come to his home for their lessons. His good wife herself had suggested it. It was small, that home, as they all knew, but with the little ones there two days a week, and those older three, they could manage. There was always a way, he told them.

It had been as he said. Although he had only one book, a worn and frayed geography, the Old Teacher had so much in his head that every school day brought new and fascinating things to Arturo and his friends. As for their having no pencils, no paper for their writing lessons — well, the ground was smooth and soft behind the house. On pleasant days they practiced their writing there with sharpened sticks. Yes, there was always a way.

Then the food had come. Arturo was sure he would never forget how delicious that first bowl of hot soup tasted, how good the cup of milk was. Everyone had been especially excited about the milk, for it was made from powder by the women whose turn it was that day. Mixed with water, simmered a bit over the fire, then cooled — there it was, good milk. Who would have thought it?

When Arturo got home that afternoon, his grandmother had cried for joy that the good lunches had begun. At first, that is. When he told her about the milk made from powder, she frowned.

"What did you say?" she asked sharply.

Arturo had explained as best he could, but with each word she became more angry until, "You shall not drink it!" she cried. "It is another trick, a stranger's trick. Poison, it is. Poison powder!"

Nothing that Arturo said then was of any use. She was right. She knew she was right. Let the other young ones take sick and die, but not her Arturo, the only one left of all her family. Fourteen summers had he seen. And why? Because she, his grandmother, had found food for him all during the fighting in ways she did not now care to remember. Had she done this only to have him leave her because of powder from a stranger? No!

"Say it!" she had demanded. "Say the promise that you will touch not one drop of the poison milk!" And Arturo had said it.

Next day was for the little ones at school, but those older came for the lunch as the Old Teacher had arranged. As soon as Arturo arrived, he could tell from the way the women looked at him that his grandmother had been talking to them, too, about the poison powder. Not being able to drink the milk, even having the women know would not have been so bad, although that was bad enough, if only the other boys had not heard about it. But they had, and at recess time they were lying in wait for him.

"Poor weak little Arturo," they taunted. "Mustn't drink the milk." And they called his grandmother a stupid, a know-nothing.

They had been careful not to say it when the Old Teacher was near by, though, and Arturo understood that. The Old Teacher believed the milk to be good. His grandmother's calling it poison meant she no longer trusted him.

For two days he had endured it, until yesterday afternoon, when the Old Teacher, coming unexpectedly around the corner of the house, had overheard the taunts and the jeers. He had passed by, then, with only a smile for them, but when school was over he asked Arturo to remain behind.

"What is your trouble, my boy?" he asked. "Is it the same that has brought the unhappiness to your eyes for two days now, when you have thought I did not see?"

Arturo nodded, but did not reply.

"Speak," said the Old Teacher firmly. "I must know what it is, Arturo."

"It is the milk," said Arturo. "The milk made from the powder. My grandmother will not allow me to drink it."

The Old Teacher was puzzled. "But you said you did not like it."

"That was not true," Arturo told him unhappily. "I drank it the first day and found it good. But my grandmother considers it poison. She says all who drink it will take sick and die. She made me promise not to take it. And she has——"

"I see," interrupted the Old Teacher. "She has not hesitated to pass her opinion along to all. To all, that is, excepting only myself and my good wife. I am surprised no one told me, surprised that you kept silent, Arturo."

"It was because you said the milk was good," explained Arturo. "Because we thought that if——"

Again the Old Teacher interrupted. "I understand, my boy. You did not wish to hurt me. Come, we go to your grandmother together."

They found his grandmother sitting under the big tree in front of the house, staring off into the distance. She greeted the Old Teacher with dignity, but not gladly, and Arturo could see the great worry in her eyes.

When first the Old Teacher started to speak, she looked away, her lips set in a determined line. Ignoring her aloofness, the Old Teacher talked on, about the kind friends who were sending the food to the young of their village. As yet he did not fully understand just how they had come to do so, how they had known about them there in the mountains. It was partly because of their own government in Rome, that he knew. Partners, the stranger had called them. Well, in time he would have the whole story. Then he would let all know just how this had come to pass.

Gradually Arturo's grandmother relaxed, turning to look into the Old Teacher's eyes. But when he mentioned the powder for the making of milk, she stiffened. "No!" she cried. "My Arturo shall not drink of it!"

"Have I ever told you that which was not so, old friend?" the Old Teacher asked gently. "I say to you, it is not poison. The kind, far-distant friends who have sent it are honorable. For three days now our young have drunk of the milk made from the powder. Not one has become sick. Already their eyes are more bright. But it is not our young alone who have been helped. In all our land others have been drinking the milk. Nor has any died of it."

The old woman was silent, her gnarled fingers twisting the corner of her threadbare apron.

"Would you keep this good from your Arturo? Just how the powder that is dry can have come from milk that is wet is something else I do not as yet fully understand. But I believe, and I ask you to do the same — for your Arturo."

To Arturo, sitting on the ground under the big tree, it seemed that his grandmother would never reply. But at last, her eyes swimming with tears, her hands trembling, she said, "My Arturo may drink of the milk made from the powder."

The Old Teacher laid his hand affectionately upon her shoulder. "You have decided well, old friend. And now there is something more I would ask of you. The man who delivers the food will soon also bring that which is

ONLY AN IMPROVISED HUT BY THE ROADSIDE, BUT GOOD FOOD WAS THERE FOR THE
TEEN-AGERS AND CHILDREN OF THE GREEK VILLAGE OF CASTORIA

THE YOUNG
REFUGEES
IN PALESTINE
WERE NOT
FORGOTTEN

needed to make bread. The women will then bake it in their homes, taking it to our school for the lunches. Will not you, whose bread has always been best of all, take charge of the breadmakers?"

Again Arturo's grandmother stiffened, this time in dismay. "No! No!"

"It is for our young," the Old Teacher said. "There will be more strength for them in the bread if it is made carefully and rightly."

Again the gnarled fingers twisted the apron's corner. Again there was a long silence until, "I shall do it for our young," she told him in a thin quavering voice. And throwing the apron over her head, she ran into the house.

Which is why Arturo hastened eagerly toward school and the other boys. Who was it the Old Teacher had chosen from among all the women to take charge of the breadmakers? She whom they had called an old stupid, a know-nothing. His grandmother.

The skim-milk powder for the teen-agers and children there in Arturo's Italian village was part of the plan made by UNICEF's executive board members when they began their work.

It was not easy for them to answer that question: "What shall the Fund do first?" How could they choose those in greatest need when hundreds of thousands of young people and children needed medical care — at once? When hundreds of thousands needed clothes — at once. And shelter. And food.

Food — no matter what else each young person, each child lacked, all needed food. To send food first was therefore the board's decision. But where? Those in the war-devastated countries of Europe were hungry, those in Asia and the islands of the Pacific. But a start must be made somewhere, and because the food could be gotten most quickly to those in Europe, to begin in Europe was the board's second decision.

Another question immediately presented itself. *What* food? Not only must it be that which had in it the greatest possible amount of nourishment, it must be that which could readily be shipped across oceans, and, without spoiling, readily transported on land. It must be food that the Fund could buy in large quantities and as cheaply as possible, for every dollar must be stretched.

For the answer to this question UNICEF turned to the nutrition experts of FAO and WHO. A special United Nations team was then appointed by these Specialized Agencies, a Nutrition Committee all of whom had spent many years in the field of youth and child care. Its members were men and women from twelve countries: Canada, China, Cuba, Czechoslovakia, France, Great Britain, Greece, Hungary, Italy, Norway, Poland, and the United States. Those representing the United States were from the U. S. Public Health Service and the Children's Bureau in Washington.

Quickly these experienced men and women gave their answer: "Send milk, skim milk in powdered form; cheese; cod-liver oil; fats; meat and fish; cocoa; beans and peas; jam and sugar; peanut butter."

What countries had these foods on hand to sell to the Fund? By telephone, by cable, by air mail the inquiry went out around the world. By telephone, by cable, by air mail the replies came back, and the prices quoted were generously low. The orders that the Fund then placed were almost unbelievably large. Within three years UNICEF was to buy from the United States alone more than two hundred and forty-five million pounds of the skim-milk powder, enough to make several billion cups of milk.

Even before the orders were sent out, those of UNICEF realized that no matter how much food the Fund could buy, it would not be enough for the undernourished youth who were waiting. That there were many more than anyone had dreamed they now knew, for letters were arriving from the governments of the war-devastated European countries.

With all its plans, the United Nations has one requirement. No UN project is launched in any country unless the people of that country, through their government, invite the UN experts to come to them for that particular purpose. So, now, with UNICEF. As soon as the executive board made its decision to start work in the war-devastated countries of Europe, word of that decision had gone out to the governments there.

"Do you wish us to come to you?" the cables asked.

"Come as soon as you can," replied Albania, Austria, Bulgaria, Czechoslovakia, Finland, Greece, Hungary, Italy, Poland, Romania, and Yugoslavia. Later, after the drought of 1947, France joined them.

"*Portrzeba nam wiecej zywnosci,*" cabled Poland. "We need more food."

In order to know how much food to ship to each country, UNICEF sent Dr. Martha Eliot, then Associate Director of the U. S. Children's Bureau, later Assistant Director-General of WHO, to the various countries, where she asked the government officials how many of their young people and children were undernourished. She asked them about the amount of food they themselves could supply, what the voluntary agencies were doing. With each of the reports Dr. Eliot brought back was a promise. "We will be responsible for distributing, preparing, and serving to our boys and girls all the food that you send," said the governments. "And we will match it in amount with what we have or can produce."

It was the start of a partnership between the Fund and the people of each country through their government, which was to become ever more important as time passed. In each of the European countries the people matched or more than matched the amount of food UNICEF sent them. In addition, government and volunteer staffs carried on the work at the food-distributing centers.

It was difficult for the government officials to give Dr. Eliot even an approximation of the number of children and teen-agers who were in greatest need of the Fund's help. The wanderers, the homeless ones—who could say how many there were? But they did their best, and when the figures were added at UNICEF's headquarters, the Secretariat was appalled that the total reached into the millions.

But with this cruel evidence of the suffering caused to youth by the world's most terrible war there was word which was inspiring to everyone. Already many volunteers in every country were offering to lend a hand — groups of teachers and doctors, members of parents' organizations, and hundreds of individual citizens, such as cooks, warehousemen, and truck drivers. What the various voluntary organizations were doing was also stirring — the International Red Cross, CARE, the Boy Scout International Bureau, the World Association of Girl Guides and Girl Scouts, the Friends' Service Committee, the International Lions and Rotary Clubs, the International Y.M.C.A. and Y.W.C.A., World Catholic, Jewish, and Protestant organizations, international labor organizations. And the organizations of Europe, the Don Suisse of Switzerland, the Red Crescent, and many others. Now the United Nations International Children's Emergency Fund was joining them.

Plans for shipping the food were quickly worked out. In each country it would go to one central place, usually the capital, where an official representative of the Fund would be on hand to help in forwarding it to the waiting young people and children. To those in the large cities and in remote villages. To those in mountain passes, by the sea, and on vast and lonely plains. How could this be done when the UNICEF partners were faced with the same bombed-out railroads, wrecked bridges, broken-down trucks that handicapped the workers of IRO? Determination was the answer here, too. And determination won the victory, even by dogcart.

Milk bars were set up first, in schools, orphanages, hospitals, churches, and other public buildings. If none of these was available, improvised huts were made to do in fields and by roadsides, even though there was barely enough room for a stove and a table, barely enough shelter for the babies, the small children, and young mothers who came. All too often stoves could be found only after long and frantic search. Kettles in which to process the skim-milk powder were more than difficult to come by. Everywhere there was a shortage of fuel. But the milk bars were opened.

"At seven-thirty we women volunteers arrive to heat the milk and get things in order," wrote one of the workers. "We put a fair-sized amount of bread behind scenes for those whose mothers cannot supply it. At seven forty-five the children begin to come. Very young they are, mostly babies really, with their mothers or fathers or older brothers and sisters bringing them. They pass in line, the babies holding up their cups for a generous ladleful of the hot milk.

"I have seen many children carry the hot milk to seats behind the crowd, and there sit quietly warming their cold little hands on the side of the cup. They come eagerly or shyly for seconds, and many a piece of bread made by our volunteers in their own homes finds its way from our bags into the hands of children who want it but do not ask. Some of the unemployed fathers stay and help us to clean up after the children are gone."

While the milk bars were getting under way, food was already arriving for the teen-agers. Again, in an unbelievably short time, in schools, orphanages, and the other centers, many thousands were passing in front of serving tables, there to be given a meal to which the Fund had contributed half, their own government half. Very simple those meals were — milk, bread, and soup. Or stew and a cup of milk. But how welcome!

During the first winter the number of feeding stations in Europe reached thirty thousand, with the Fund partners planning, preparing, and serving three and a half million meals a day. You know the work it is for your mother to plan, market for, and cook three meals a day for your family. Even with the grocery and the meat market near by, one thousand ninety-five meals a year is a big job. For every one of the three and a half million meals served each day by the UNICEF partners, food had to be found and bought around the world. It had to be shipped across oceans, then delivered and cooked and served.

It was a remarkable partnership, a great United Nations team at work in all kinds of ways. Mothers joined in community breadmaking projects in hundreds of communities. Teen-age girls helped cook UNICEF meals as part of their school cooking lessons. Teen-age boys grew vegetables and delivered them to the feeding centers. At UNICEF headquarters the Secretariat was constantly on the alert for new kinds of food to ship. When it was discovered that shark-liver oil is thirty-three times more potent than cod-liver oil, shark-liver oil from New Zealand was put into child-size capsules in Canada and shipped across the Atlantic. Coconut oil from the Philippines was processed in Czechoslovakia, then sent to other European countries, where it delighted the children as a delicious spread for their bread.

Regularly, month after month, ships arrived in European ports with ever-increasing amounts of food until, by the end of three years, the number of meals being served to the young people and children in the twelve European countries had jumped to six million a day. With the cargo, cod-liver oil for one million children in Germany was included, by agreement with the Occupation Authorities of the West Zone.

Wherever the Fund partners served food, gay posters made by teen-agers and children brightened the walls. On each poster appeared the word *UNICEF*, a word which was the same in every language, a new word all understood. At first the United Nations International Children's Emergency Fund had been translated separately into each language and dialect. The result was utter confusion in UNICEF's reports! Then someone suggested using UNICEF everywhere, and the difficulty was resolved.

When the teen-agers and children of Austria designed and painted a thousand UNICEF posters, they were proud to have them exhibited in Vienna, then sent to Lake Success and the large cities of the United States. In Czechoslovakia, where a school-poster contest was held, the winning design was chosen not only for the poster to be printed and displayed in

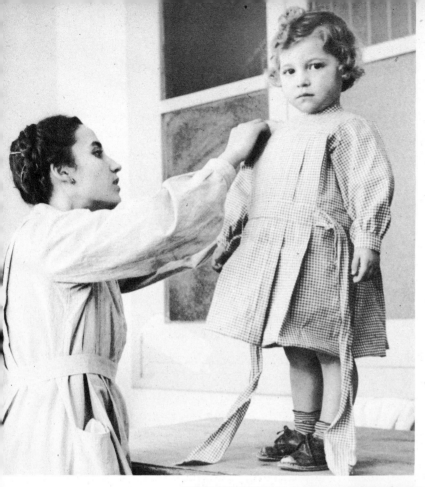

A TEEN-AGE GIRL
IN A NAPLES
ORPHANAGE
PINS IN
THE LAST TUCK
ON THE DRESS
SHE HAS MADE
FOR HER
SMALL FRIEND

A TEEN-AGE BOY
IN ATHENS
MAKES
CHILDREN'S SHOES
FROM
UNICEF LEATHER

all the Czech feeding centers, but for UNICEF's 1949 Christmas card as well. Thousands of Americans bought for their own Christmas greetings the picture painted by eight-year-old Jitka Semkova of the small Bohemian village of Rusolfov. When the judges in Prague selected it as the best, they had no idea that the lovely Maypole design done in bright, bold water colors was the work of one so young.

"It is meant to express joy," small, fair-haired Jitka explained to her teacher, Josip Bartouska, when she handed it in, "by showing children dancing around a Maypole. The wreath around the top is the sign that the line of happy children is endless."

Many of the posters showed children happily receiving shoes and clothing as well as food. These, as well as medical supplies and soap, were also now being shipped by UNICEF. For the shoes and clothing, the UNICEF partners worked out a special plan. The packages from CARE and other voluntary organizations contained very welcome ready-made clothes and shoes. To add to this supply, UNICEF shipped raw wool and cotton, and leather, from which the people in each country could make what they needed. In this way many men and women were given employment by their governments, weaving the materials, manufacturing clothing and shoes. Joining with them, thousands of volunteers also worked busily.

In Hungary men and women made shoes, boys' pants and shirts, girls' dresses and underclothes, stockings, small children's creepers, and sheets. In Czechoslovakia the raw cotton went into the material for babies' diapers, which were distributed by the baby clinics there. In Finland much of the cotton was used for flannelette, which was sent to the schools where the mothers met and made clothes for their children. And teen-agers everywhere joined in, the girls in their school sewing classes, the boys in the shoemaking.

Within four years UNICEF shipped five million dollars' worth of hides and leather, wool and cotton. Enough leather and hides for a million pairs of children's shoes. Enough raw wool for a million blankets and a million outfits of clothes.

Whenever UNICEF field representatives went out to see how things were progressing at the centers in the cities, the towns, the villages, and the countryside, they were impressed by the feeling of responsibility among the local workers. Not that everything was perfect. No work carried on by human beings is ever that. But far more often than not records were in order, as they were with the schoolmaster in UNICEF's northernmost outpost in Nuorgan, Finland, seventy degrees north latitude.

To reach Nuorgan, where about one hundred and twenty Laplanders live, the field worker had to travel by plane, boat, and truck, the same route over which the UNICEF supplies had gone. There, in the village school for twenty-four children, the schoolmaster proudly brought out his record book. Everything he had received was accounted for.

It was all part of a careful, tested organization that was to prove its worth in a sudden emergency. In the summer of 1948 word reached UNICEF headquarters from Palestine that hundreds of thousands of Arab refugees, fleeing from the fighting to the desert, were in dire straits, with little food, almost no shelter, no medicine for the sick. At once UNICEF went to work. In less than a month UNICEF supplies reached Beirut. Only two weeks later food for the small children, for those in their teens, reached refugee camps in Lebanon, Trans-Jordan, North Palestine, Syria, and Israel.

In the help then given, UNICEF worked with the United Nations Relief for Palestine Refugees, a partnership in which each contributed half. Again improvised centers were set up for serving milk to babies and small children and meals to older boys and girls wherever they could be found. In Syria hundreds were living in the catacombs under a Roman amphitheater. Others were in a dungeon carved out of the rock by the Phoenicians thousands of years ago. In Hebron the partners took over King Solomon's kitchen. The story goes that King Solomon, on a visit to Hebron, was so impressed by the devotion of the people, as well as distressed by their poverty, that he set up a fund by which daily meals were to be given to the poor and their families until the end of the world. Ever since, the people of Hebron had served meals as the king directed, later using their own money for the work. But when war came, they sadly realized that soon there would be no more food to serve. It was then that UNICEF arrived and the meals continued without a lapse.

Approximately five hundred thousand small children, youth, and young mothers in the Middle East were shortly being given nourishing food. With the food came medical supplies, shelter equipment, clothing, and blankets. Doctors and nurses made their regular rounds, and the refugee parents were most co-operative. As a result, there was no serious epidemic.

Letters of appreciation filled UNICEF's mailbags. "The Students' Organization of the National School in Oznicam, Velassko, Mezirisi, thank you with all their hearts for the help you have given us," said one. "We live in a small mountain village, and the majority of our boys and girls have very far to come to school. The good milk, butter, fats, meat tins, and cod-liver oil from you were the basis of our nutrition throughout the year. We gained 2 kilograms each on the average.

"In return, we promise to do our best to make peace between nations everlasting so that there may be no wars which are the peril of humanity. On behalf of the whole school, we thank you once more." Signed: F. Hrabovsky, Chairman. K. Kubin, Cultural Officer. M. Klanicova, Executive Secretary.

Enclosed with this letter was the following poem, here translated from the original Czech. The author did not sign his name, sending it instead in the name of "our four hundred and twenty mountaineer parents and their children."

> Honored ladies and distinguished gentlemen,
> please accept our warmest and heartfelt thanks
> for the concern that you have shown us
> for your good heart which you are extending.
>
> We thank you a hundred thousand times
> in behalf of the mountain boys and girls of Velassko,
> who from distant pastures are in great hurry to get to school
> because in school not only our minds but our bodies, too, are fed.
>
> The bread spread and tasty cocoa smell nicely all over the place,
> and on Tuesday no student is missing.
> There certainly must be a reason.
> We will give you a simple explanation
> since on that day we always have goulash soup.
>
> We are happy and proud to declare
> that we are doing well mentally and physically,
> so please accept once more our warmest thanks.
> We wish you much happiness and good fortune,
> and invite you to our country.

We, the mountaineers and children of Velassko, invite you
where birches smell with spring and the pine woods rustle merrily.
The highways will greet you with the nice smell of spring flowers
that are growing along the paths, fields, and highways.
The sky lark will sing to you.

After you have walked along the paths of Beskydy,
your soul will sparkle with brightness
as though the stars came down to decorate the earth
and speak to you of our respects and
that the children of Velassko remember you with gratitude.

In another of the envelopes was a clipping. "Bulgarian mothers owe
gratitude to UNICEF," one of them had written to her newspaper, "not only
for the material help given us, but first of all for the truth which UNICEF, by
the very fact of its being, is emphasizing — that an international union, a
United Nations organization, can and should exist."

CAMELS TOOK THE SKIM-MILK POWDER
TO THE TEEN-AGERS AND CHILDREN IN KHAN YUNIS, PALESTINE

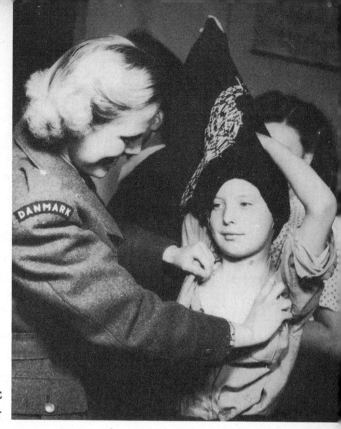

A DANISH NURSE
EXAMINES A CZECHOSLOVAKIAN BOY

THE TEAMS ARRIVE
The day had been long and hard, and the nurse was tired. But the letter must start on its way to Copenhagen tomorrow without fail. So getting out her writing pad, she set to work by the dim and flickering light of the lantern. Her hands were so cold it was difficult to guide even a pencil. But as she wrote on rapidly, she smiled. Those teen-agers, those children, how sweet they were!

"Here near Stribo," she wrote, "Dr. Lund, Miluse Humburska, the Czech social worker, and I were driving to a school in a small town. Dr. Lund was at the wheel, and the road was covered with ice and snow. All of a sudden the car skidded and fell into a ditch. At first we tried to pull it back onto the road ourselves, but we soon realized we must have help. Back we went to the town we had just passed through, and there found some farmers who offered to come with their teams to pull us out. After they had done so, one of them suggested that he drive ahead of us to show us the way. It wasn't long, though, before the road became completely impassable. So, carrying our precious equipment, we got out and walked across rough fields.

"Well, after an hour we arrived at the school where the teacher and a

YOUNG MOTHER OF BOLIVIA ON THE WAY TO THE FINE NEW CHILDREN'S HOSPITAL
LA PAZ, WHERE HER SMALL SON WILL BE GIVEN A CHECKUP

roomful of children were waiting for us. The teacher took very good care of us, inviting us into her kitchen, drying out our clothes, and giving us hot tea and a bite to eat. Then we went to work, and just as we were finishing a man brought word that about a hundred other children were stranded, because of the weather, in an inn some distance off. They had been on their way to us when they got bogged down.

" 'Please go to them,' the man begged. How could we refuse? So the teacher procured a wagon with two horses, no sled being available, and on we went. We had some sandwiches the teacher had given us but no blankets. The road was very bad, often steep and narrow, with snow piled high on both sides. We became very stiff and cold, but we got there."

There! It was finished. And she signed her name.

She was Else Andreassen of Denmark, the nurse, who with Dr. Lund and Miss Humburska made up a BCG team there in Czechoslovakia. The work of which she wrote was what hundreds of other teams, too, were doing as they traveled through the war-devastated countries of Europe. All were part of a great campaign against tuberculosis, carried on by the Scandinavian Red Cross societies, UNICEF and WHO.

The teams were called BCG because *Bacillus Calmette Guerin* was the vaccine with which they were vaccinating young people and children as a protection against tuberculosis. Developed by two French medical scientists, Drs. Calmette and Guerin, through long research before, during, and after World War I, BCG was used by the Danes and Norwegians for their youth during Nazi occupation days of World War II. It was they who laid before the United Nations the plan similarly to protect the young people and children of other European countries.

The Scandinavian BCG plan of action was simple. In the Danish and Norwegian campaigns teams of doctors and nurses went out with the necessary equipment to teen-agers and children who were first given the tuberculin test. This test, using the tuberculin which was developed by the brilliant German scientist, Dr. Robert Koch, shows in three days whether or not a person has already become infected with tuberculosis. Those of the Danish and Norwegian young people and children whose tests were negative were then vaccinated with BCG. Those with positive reactions were given X-ray and other examinations to see whether or not they had active tuberculosis. If they did, they were sent to hospitals or sanatoria.

Laboratories in Copenhagen and Oslo worked overtime producing the tuberculin and BCG vaccine. Doctors and nurses did not count the hours they worked. And as time passed they were rewarded, for the number of new TB cases among their teen-age youth and their children was proportionately less than before the campaign started.

When the war was over and word came that the children and young people in other European countries were coming down with tuberculosis by the hundreds of thousands, the gallant Danes quickly acted to give help. Through their Red Cross, their State Serum Institute, and their National Health Service, they recruited and equipped BCG field teams which as early as September 1946 went to Yugoslavia to do for the youth there what they had already done for their own young people and children. Soon they were joined by the Swedish Red Cross and the Norwegian Help-for-Europe organizations, and by 1947 Scandinavian BCG teams were at work in Austria, Czechoslovakia, Germany, Hungary, Italy, Greece, and Poland, relief made possible by contributions from the people of all three Scandinavian countries. These field teams worked valiantly. Yet so great was the emergency that all they could possibly do fell far short of the need. It was then that they turned to WHO and UNICEF of the United Nations.

"Will you not join us?" they asked.

Already WHO was actively at work on tuberculosis. One of its first steps after it was organized had been to appoint a group of tuberculosis experts to advise with the governments of the world on all aspects of this terrible disease, its prevention, and its cure. When, therefore, the Scandinavian plan was laid before the members of WHO's executive board, they saw in it an opportunity not only to help young victims of the war, but also to advance its studies of BCG itself. They voted to join the campaign. UNICEF's board, too, was in favor of it, and fortunately UNICEF had funds on hand so that a large campaign could be launched at once.

Again partnership agreements were made, with WHO providing the technical assistance of its experts, with the Scandinavians sending the teams of doctors and nurses; UNICEF and the governments, the supplies and equipment. The governments also promised to pay all local costs, to arrange for workers to travel ahead of the teams to explain what the BCG plan was and to provide interpreters to accompany the doctors and the nurses. Not one of the partners was to fail.

Dr. Esther Ammundsen of the Danish Red Cross was made chief of Field Operations. Under her direction doctors and nurses for the BCG teams were recruited first in Scandinavia, then in all the countries to which the teams went: Albania, Bulgaria, Czechoslovakia, Finland, Greece, Hungary, Italy, Poland, Romania, Yugoslavia, and the British and American zones of Germany. In each country the Scandinavians worked with the new recruits until they were experienced enough to carry on by themselves.

Cars bought in many countries and the necessary medical supplies were shipped to Europe for the teams. At first each team's equipment was necessarily very simple. But as time went on, the cars for cities and large centers carried as many as two doctors, one nurse, one laboratory specialist, one X-ray specialist, one administrator, and one driver for the X-ray truck, as well as their equipment.

The BCG vaccine presented a problem, since it must be used a short time after it is produced in the laboratory. So a plane was bought, which made regular trips from the Danish Serum Institute in Copenhagen, where the vaccine was made, to Warsaw, Prague, Bratislava (Slovakia), Budapest, Belgrade, and back. Every inch of space was packed on every trip, not only with the BCG vaccine and the tuberculin, but with penicillin, streptomycin, needles, syringes, automobile tires and spare parts, not to mention a doctor or two when there was room. Later a C-47 was lent by the United States Air Forces.

And the teams went out. To the children and young people in large cities, in towns, in villages, in the countryside. To the centers where boys and girls were gathered, the schools, the nurseries, orphanages, and hospitals. What the doctors and nurses then encountered was what doctors and nurses meet everywhere in all vaccination work, some children kicking and biting, others thoroughly enjoying the experience.

One small boy had such a good time with his tuberculin test that he cajoled a friend into relinquishing his card. Back our young hero went then for another injection, and the nurse was so busy she did not recognize him. On his third trip, however, she caught him!

At one school, after each of the boys had been given a pink or a blue card, according to the results of the test, the doctor found a lively football game going on outside, the Pinks against the Blues. Nurse Karen Giersaa, testing the children of a rural school near Novagradiska, Yugoslavia, took

THIS BCG CAR SKIDDED THROUGH MILES OF MUD TO GET TO THE BOYS AND GIRLS HERE IN THE REMOTE VILLAGE OF FNILAN, YUGOSLAVIA

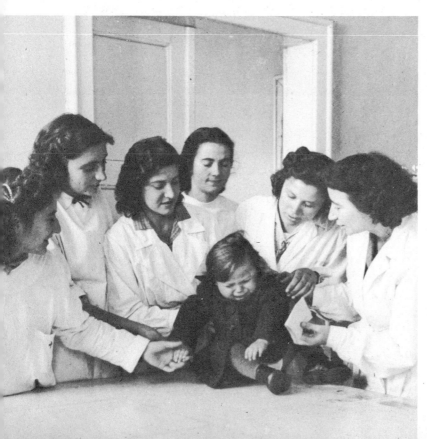

DR. KRISTINI
STANKEVIC
OF KRAGY-JEVAC,
SERBIA,
RELIES ON
HER TEEN-AGE
HELPERS IN HER
CHILDREN'S
CLINIC

each child onto her lap for the treatment. In the waiting line a seventeen-year-old young man carefully watched the procedure. When his turn came, solemnly he, too, sat down on the nurse's lap.

Day after day, week after week, the BCG teams carried on. All worked long hours, with some of the doctors and nurses in the large cities giving as many as a thousand vaccinations in one day. Despite the splendid way in which Red Cross workers and volunteers described to parents just what the campaign was for, time must often be spent by the teams in further explanation. Language, too, was a difficulty. Sometimes the interpreters were forced to be away and the teams had to manage with the few words and phrases they had picked up. In a crowded schoolroom in Poland, a Danish nurse meant to say, "Please stand in line." What she really said, to the children's great glee, was, "Everybody stand on top of each other."

"On our way through Yugoslavia we went through cities, towns, and villages," John Buntzen, a member of the first BCG team to go out from his native Denmark, wrote to UNICEF. "Everywhere we saw the destruction caused by the war, but we also saw the really amazing repair work already under way. Everybody was helping, and in one place a group of boys between the ages of thirteen and sixteen was at work rebuilding a railroad.

"Many of the cities looked more like large villages with one main street and farm buildings cluttered along both sides. The farmers kept their animal stock there at night, taking them out to the fields for the day. You can imagine the terrific jams we ran into early in the morning and again at evening, with cattle, oxcarts, teams, and all kinds of conveyances in the street.

"In remote sections, where many of the people cannot read and write, the only way we had of letting them know what we were there to do was by word of mouth. Drumbeaters went out to announce the time and place of our vaccination work. If this did not bring them in, someone from the local Yugoslav Red Cross chapter would go from house to house. So we managed, with good results. In Sombor, for instance, we reached ninety per cent of the young people there.

"I wish you could see our dispensary at work. The mothers and fathers who bring their children to us frequently come from miles away. Often they have to start in the middle of the night in order to get to our station before closing time, traveling by oxcart or horse-drawn wagon, or even walking. Since they are to be away for such a long time, they bring along the whole family, their firewood and their food. The expedition is like a picnic to them, with the added attraction of being put under the machine (the X-ray equipment) which many of them firmly believe will cure all kinds of ailments.

"Tuberculosis has always been one of the worst diseases in Yugoslavia, but since the war the death rate from TB has gone up to three hundred or more in every one hundred thousand people here."

Two years after the European BCG campaign was begun, more than fourteen million young people and children in nine countries had been given the tuberculin test. Of these, some seven and a half million had received the BCG vaccination.

Everywhere the doctors, nurses, and other team members had been welcomed as the friends that they were. In the summer their jeeps and trucks had been decorated with flowers. Songs greeted them. Gifts were showered upon them. The morning after her grandchildren were vaccinated, an old woman in Romania arrived carrying a huge bundle of rags. Setting it down upon the ground, she gingerly unwound the rags, then took out one egg for the nurse.

Children brought their crude little homemade toys to their new friends. Parents, family heirlooms — beautifully woven aprons and caps, even silver cups. At a Polish school a nine-year-old boy presented the doctor with one of his paintings, a picture of a ship arriving at Gdansk from Denmark. Above the ship waved Polish and Danish flags, with a syringe hovering protectingly over both.

To the thousands of young people and children whom the special tests showed to have active tuberculosis, hospital care was given wherever possible. There, too, UNICEF helped. Hundreds of X-ray machines arrived, tons of needed drugs, including the remarkable new drug, streptomycin, discovered by the distinguished Dr. Selman A. Waksman, head of the Microbiology Department of Rutgers University in New Brunswick, New Jersey. In a short while UNICEF shipped enough streptomycin for thirty hospitals in ten countries. To one country alone, Poland, it sent X-ray machines and other equipment sufficient for a hundred and fifty-two dispensaries.

As soon as the BCG work in Europe was well under way, WHO and UNICEF made plans for extending the campaign to other continents. When North Africa was decided upon as the next step, doctors from Algeria, Morocco, and Tunisia were chosen to go to Europe to see the work in action and there to receive training. Later those in Egypt and Tangiers joined in, as well as in Israel, Lebanon, and Syria.

Soon reports were arriving from these teams in the field. "I carry on my work in the palace of the Sultan, in the market places, and in front of the mosques," wrote Dr. Max Pellet from Marrakech, Morocco. "I never saw such crowds! But my biggest difficulty is not with the young people and the children and their parents but with the wind that knocks over my alcohol sterilizing lamp, that blows my papers away and sends sand into my eyes and over all my equipment."

Out across the desert sped word from the Sultan about the BCG teams, to the caids, on down to the chirs, then to the village chieftains. It was amazing to the doctors and nurses to see how quickly the news spread. Dr. Claud Simon, assigned to the extreme south of Morocco, found tribesmen and their children waiting at each oasis to welcome him and his team.

Each BCG car in Africa carried either a refrigerator or thermos containers to keep the BCG vaccine fresh. Each had camping equipment as well as an assortment of tools. They needed it all. "During our first three months in Morocco," wrote Dr. Jean Michel Millet, whose team was composed of two nurses, two Arab assistants, and a chauffeur, "our biggest obstacle was the rains that flooded and cut the trails. Sometimes we had to detour for as much as a hundred miles, and even repair the primitive road ourselves. But despite everything, we managed to cover from fifty to a hundred kilometers a day in the districts of Taradan, Tiznit, and Inezgan.

"There is a lot of superstition here which also holds us up. Nevertheless, it is amazing how the people come to understand what we are doing. And there is a great deal of appreciation, too. Always, at the end of our work in a place, somehow they manage to give us a *diffa*, a big feast with countless courses, including their main dish, mutton cooked in sand. Couscous, honey fritters, and mint tea are the dessert. Afterward the men play the tam-tam to us while the women sing shrill music, or we are entertained with snake dances in which cobras, pythons, and vipers are sometimes a little too close for comfort!"

Busy though UNICEF's board and UNICEF's Secretariat were with the thousands of feeding stations in Europe and the Middle East, with the

EVERY GIRL IN VICTORIA COLLEGE, PATIALA, INDIA, TOOK THE TUBERCULIN TEST
FOR TB, ADMINISTERED BY A SCANDINAVIAN-UNICEF TEAM OF DOCTORS AND NURSES

FRENCH DOCTORS AND NURSES EXAMINE THE YOUTH OF THE NOMADES OF TUNISIA

BCG teams and all their other work, they did not forget the young people and children of Asia, where half the youth of the world live. At the very time that the BCG teams were making their European rounds, a UNICEF team of two was traveling through Burma, Indo-China, Indonesia, Pakistan, the Philippines, and the United Kingdom territories of Hongkong, Singapore, North Borneo, Sarawak, and Brunei. The members of that team were Dr. Thomas Parran, former Surgeon-General of the U. S. Public Health Service, and Dr. C. K. Laksmanan, director of the All-India Institute of Hygiene and Public Health in Calcutta.

In each place they visited, they talked with government and public-health officials about their youth. They talked with teachers, with missionaries of all faiths, and with others working among boys and girls. And they went out to the young people and children themselves, in their homes and their schools.

What did they find? "Hunger is the constant companion of young people everywhere in Asia," they reported to UNICEF. "Hunger and disease, with malaria the most serious but with yaws taking its toll." Yaws is the disfiguring skin disease of the rural tropics, which ultimately affects the bones as well.

Upon Dr. Parran's return UNICEF's executive board met with him in Paris to decide what to do. Before them, from all the countries the team had visited in Asia, were eager requests for UNICEF to enter into partnership with them. But all the money in the Fund was not enough to provide food for the millions of young people and children in Asia who were hungry, to give them the medical care they needed.

The decision the board members made then was important to youth around the world, for the plan they worked out was for the future as well as today in Asia. It was to be repeated in Latin America, in Europe, wherever UNICEF would go. That plan was this: country by country to meet with the governments to discuss long-range plans for their youth. All the board knew that such plans meant the work of many years. Yet only in this way could conditions be made permanently better.

But first the after-war emergency must be met so far as was possible among the suffering young people and children in Asia. Once again, then, the ships and planes arrived, loaded with food and medical supplies from UNICEF, bound for such emergency places as the port cities in China including Shanghai, Nanking, Peiping, Canton, and Hankow; for the refugee camps in India and Pakistan; for the boys and girls in Jogjakarta, Indonesia; for those on the island of Lombok, where conditions were especially pitiable. The youth of Japan had their share, too. By arrangement with the Supreme Commander of the Allied Powers, more than three million pounds of skim-milk powder were sent there for more than a hundred and thirty-eight thousand babies and children, together with enough cotton to make material for more than four hundred and sixty thousand teen-agers' and children's suits of clothes. In Ceylon, India, and Pakistan, BCG teams arrived and promptly set to work.

As the long lines of mothers and babies came to the milk bars, as older boys and girls passed by serving tables for their lunches, their government officials were conferring with UNICEF on the long-range plans for them. Some of the governments already had such nation-wide plans for their young people and children. Their splendidly trained doctors and public-health nurses were ready to train others if only more clinics, more health centers, and more hospitals could be established. Other governments asked for help in working out what would be most effective in caring for their youth over a period of years. Across the Pacific Ocean, in Latin America, the government officials were also conferring with UNICEF in the same way.

The number of young people and children who needed help on these two continents alone was staggering — more than four hundred million of them under sixteen years of age in Asia, more than fifty-one million under fifteen in Latin America, and a high proportion undernourished. Could any organization, even one as large and well organized as UNICEF, even begin to help? Yes, UNICEF could do just that. It could begin. Going over the long-range plans, it asked each government to say what it wished to do first. In making these answers, the governments also had the help of specialists from FAO and WHO, who arrived to give their advice.

The answers varied, but no government asked for anything it was able to do for itself. And each pledged to match or more than match what the Fund might give. "We wish to start by fighting the diseases that are attacking so many of our young people and children." "We wish to set up demonstration feeding centers where our parents and health workers may learn how to give our youth more healthful meals from the food we are producing." "We wish to send teams out into our rural regions to teach our young people, our children, and their parents better health habits." "We wish to add to our hospital accommodations for our youth." "We wish to train more doctors and other health workers as soon as we can."

Country by country, the fight against disease — and teams in large areas of Indonesia, in all of Haiti, carrying on great campaigns against yaws. All the teams have penicillin supplied by UNICEF, for it has been learned that an injection or two of that drug brings a cure of yaws.

Country by country, demonstration feeding centers — and teams arriving at twenty-four government schools in Honduras where the pupils are given carefully planned lunches. Parents, doctors, health workers, and teachers come to see how the health of the boys and girls is improving with the milk and the other protective foods which UNICEF provides and with the vegetables, the fruit, and the like that have been grown in Honduras. Members of the country's National Committee for the Protection of the Child also come, for they have joined the UNICEF-government teams in plans to establish demonstration feeding centers in other schools throughout Honduras.

Country by country, better use of the food that is produced — and UNICEF-FAO-government teams in seven countries of Europe building skim-milk powder processing plants so that during the seasons when milk is abundant, powder is made and young people and children then have milk to drink the rest of the year.

Country by country, better health habits taught to youth and their parents — and teams arriving in the rural regions of India in vans equipped with radios, projectors, and films as well as with scales, thermometers, needles and syringes, soap, and disinfectants. Wherever the films are shown, Walt Disney's are more popular than any others! The same kinds of team arriving in the Temuco and Aconcagua districts of Chile. Arriving in the Philippines with a child health specialist and a public-health consultant who will stay for a year in the new center that has been built for rural health work and where the Filipino workers will be trained to carry on in the future.

Country by country, more hospitals for youth — in Bolivia a young people's and children's hospital at La Paz, which is the first of its kind in the country and to which UNICEF sends supplies and equipment. A hospital where two hundred young persons and children are cared for at one time, where the doctors, nurses, and health workers who are trained go into other parts of Bolivia as well as staying to work in the new hospital.

IT'S UNICEF MILK TIME
AT THIS INDIAN SCHOOL
IN SOLOLA, GUATEMALA,
WHERE AN ALBINO GIRL
IS A REAL RARITY
— AND IN TOKYO
NURSERY SCHOOL CHILDREN
SMILE THEIR THANKS
FOR THE GOOD MILK, RICE,
AND VEGETABLES

Country by country, better-trained health workers for youth — and refresher courses for those in many parts of Europe whose opportunities for further study were interrupted by the war, and doctors, nurses, and others arriving in France, Sweden, Switzerland, and the United Kingdom where these courses are given.

Dr. Kristini Stankevic in her Serbian town of Kragy-jevac knows how much these refresher courses mean, for she attended one of them. During the war no one in Kragy-jevac worked more tirelessly than she in caring for the young people and children there. Among the many things she did was to start a crèche where she trained teen-age girls to help her. When the letter arrived saying she had been chosen for a refresher course in Sweden, she left happily. And as soon as she returned, she put her new knowledge to work. Today she is chief pediatrician not only of her own town but of all the surrounding district. Even her fourteen-hour day seems too short for all that she does. She runs the crèche. She directs a mothers' dispensary. To her training of her teen-age helpers she has added a course for nurses and one for doctors. In the doctorless villages of her district she meets with mothers to show them how to care better for their children.

Country by country, UNICEF fellowships awarded — and men and women going abroad to colleges, universities, medical and other special schools for courses in youth health work. Throughout the United Nations many such fellowships are given to those working in many fields. When UNESCO published a book about them, *Study Abroad,* upward of twenty thousand were listed. Of these, UNICEF has its share.

Among the many schools and universities where the UNICEF fellows are studying is the great health center in Calcutta which is under the direction of the All-India Institute of Hygiene and Public Health and which UNICEF has helped develop. Here doctors, nurses, and others whose specialty is the care of youth come from all parts of Southeast Asia for the courses that make them of greater usefulness.

In Paris the International Children's Center, which UNICEF helped make possible, has students from around the world, with UNICEF fellows among them each year. There the best that medical science has learned about the care of young people and children is assembled. There, the year around, specialists from many countries give courses to men and women from many countries. There scientists carry on important research for youth.

Such was the work of three and a half years that UNICEF reported to the General Assembly of the United Nations. Work done in eleven countries and six territories in Asia. In fourteen countries in Europe. In seventeen countries in Latin America. In eight countries in the Middle East. In five countries in North Africa. And UNICEF teams arriving for youth around the world.

THE GIRLS OF THE CAVTAT CHILDREN'S
HOME IN YUGOSLAVIA SINGING A WELCOME TO THEIR UNICEF FRIENDS

ANDROMACHE TSONGAS, GREEK GOVERNMENT NUTRITIONIST, MEETS IN ATHENS
WITH HER FAO TEAM TO PLAN FOR MORE AND BETTER FOOD FOR GREEK YOUTH

4-H CLUB MEMBERS AT WASHINGTON, D.C., BOUND FOR EUROPEAN FARMS
TO LIVE AND WORK AS PART OF THE INTERNATIONAL FARM YOUTH EXCHANGE

A SWEDISH FORESTRY
STUDENT WORKS ON POLLINIZATION

BREAD IS PEACE

It was evening in the beautiful Aztec garden of the Pan American Union in Washington, D.C. Gathered under the trees and beside the lovely flower beds was a large group of youth, come together for a 4-H Club candlelighting ceremony. Four candles, lighted by four young people, in token of the 4-H purpose — Head, Heart, Hand, and Health for the service of mankind. With them, then, a fifth candle brightly glowed for International Understanding and Friendship, and all in the garden joined hands as they pledged to work for world peace and the mutual exchange of information.

The youth in the Aztec garden that June evening in 1950 were delegates to the first such international meeting of young agriculturalists. Those from forty-seven states of the United States and Puerto Rico were 4-H Club members. Others, including those from Finland, came from groups with the same 4-H name. Those from England represented the Young Farmers' Organization, which has many members in Scotland, Ireland, and Wales, as well as in England. But differences in name did not matter. Much more important was the fact that all seventy-six of those from abroad, from fourteen different countries, including Denmark, France, Germany, Norway, and Sweden, were busy with the same kinds of projects, each in his or her country, on their home farms. Busy raising corn, vegetables, fruit. Busy with their cows, pigs, and sheep; with their home canning and freezing.

Those from abroad had just come from visits on American farms where they had been guests of 4-H Club members and their families, and had worked with them there. At the same time, American visitors had been abroad on *their* farms as guests, all of it part of the International Farm Youth Exchange plan which in 1948 was launched by the Extension Division of the United States Department of Agriculture.

As the delegates attended the meetings in Washington they had thrilled to the thought of still other clubs like theirs around the world. They had heard about the 5-S club in India, five because the Hindu language needs that many words to express 4-H. The 5-S symbol is the lotus bud, instead of the 4-H four-leaf clover, but it means the same to Indian youth. The delegates had learned that in Argentina there are more than a thousand *Pais* clubs, as they are called. That the youth in Brazil, Peru, Uruguay, and Venezuela have their agricultural organizations; those in Cuba, Haiti, and the Virgin Islands theirs. That there are many hundred Junior Farmers' Clubs in Australia, New South Wales, and Rhodesia. That in South Korea, when the United States Occupation troops suggested the 4-H plan to the Korean young people, more than thirty thousand of them organized more than a thousand clubs within a short time.

Talking things over in Washington, the young agriculturalists had quickly discovered that although their home farms differed in many ways, nevertheless they were all facing the same problems — taking care of the soil, getting the best kinds of seed, fighting insect pests, keeping rats away from their stored grain. If they raised animals, what breeds to buy, what to feed them, what to do when they became sick.

It was interesting to hear how the various governments were helping, for all the delegates had such help, in one way or another. Those in the United States have their county agents, who attend their meetings, who stop by to see how things are going with their 4-H projects, and who, as part of each state's agricultural college, represent the United States Department of Agriculture in Washington. It was because of their friends, the county agents, that the American young people clearly understood just what was meant when they were told that the Food and Agriculture Organization of the United Nations is "the county agent of the world."

To their happiness that they, young agriculturalists, now had an international organization was added the inspiring thought that for the rest of their lives they would be together in FAO. Already many of the young delegates were planning for farms of their own in the years ahead. By that time they would be too old for membership in an international youth organization. But FAO would remain, their special part of the United Nations, ready to help them through their governments. And for them their 4-H motto would always be linked with that of FAO. FAO's: *Fiat panis — Let there be bread.* That of the 4-H Clubs, *Make the best, better.*

FAO had its beginnings in May, 1943, when at the invitation of President Franklin D. Roosevelt, representatives from forty-four nations met at Hot Springs, Virginia, where they agreed to work together "so that hunger may be banished from the earth and that a stable world agriculture may be established."

That there would be an after-war food emergency they knew. And they made plans to meet it. But the food problem of the world had existed long before World War II. The delegates recognized the fact that basically the peoples of the world had always been and still were divided into two parts — those who have enough to eat, and those who never get enough for health and growth. Millions upon millions of youth, of children, who have never known what it is like not to be hungry, even though two thirds of the world's workers are farmers. Less than a billion who have enough food, more than a billion who do not. Plans to increase the amount of food grown in the world were also discussed at Hot Springs.

When on October 16, 1945, at Quebec, thirty-four nations signed its charter through their representatives, FAO came into being. Within five years the number of FAO's member nations was to reach sixty-three, with yet more nations already applying for admission. All of them working together to carry out FAO's purpose, as written in its charter: "To help nations raise the standards of living. To improve the nutrition of all countries. To increase the efficiency of farming, forestry, and fisheries. And through all these means to widen the opportunity of all the peoples for productive work."

The way in which FAO was then organized to carry out this great task made it the forerunner of WHO, UNESCO, and the other Specialized Agencies, for they were to be similarly set up.

FAO has a General Conference made up of one voting delegate from each of its member nations. It meets annually to review progress and to decide on special projects for the coming year. FAO has an executive board, often called the "World Food Council," whose eighteen members come from as many countries. The FAO Council meets several times in the course of each year, carrying out the projects upon which the General Conference has decided. FAO has a Secretariat, headed by a Director-General, its executive chief. And for right-hand aides in most of its member countries, FAO has National FAO Committees, made up of government officials and citizens who have agricultural interests and specialties. These committees keep in touch with their farmers, their agricultural organizations and schools, and spread word of FAO's activities and publications.

FAO's first Director-General was Sir John Boyd Orr, now Lord Boyd Orr, a brilliant Scot widely known for his important research in nutrition. It was Sir John who said: "Hunger is at the heart of the world's troubles. Unless people are fed, the best treaties and agreements can come to nothing." Adding what is today a watchword of FAO workers everywhere: "Bread is peace."

FAO's job is mainly the long-range problem of helping the farmers the world over to raise more and better food. But in the postwar years, when there were grave shortages of food in many countries, FAO had to do something at once to prevent widespread starvation. Voluntarily, FAO member countries got together as an international emergency food council and allocated the foods and supplies, such as fertilizers, to the various countries on the basis of need, not ability to pay high prices for the scarce items. FAO member governments agreed to limit the feeding of livestock for a time so that more food would be available for human beings. Timber was also scarce, and Europe needed wood to rebuild homes and factories after the war. At an FAO conference in Czechoslovakia, governments agreed to increase the cutting of timber by ten per cent. FAO specialists went to various countries to help restore farming quickly.

At the same time that FAO was exerting devoted effort in this after-war emergency, it started its work so that the peoples of the world would have more food in the years to come. Specialists in many agricultural fields were chosen for FAO's Secretariat, men and women willing to leave their own countries in order to serve the United Nations.

Just as the county agents help 4-H Club members with expert advice, so FAO's Secretariat is constantly at the service of agricultural organizations and college faculties and of individual citizens through their governments. Day after day hundreds of letters with their hundreds of questions arrive at FAO's temporary World Headquarters in Washington, D.C., and each is carefully answered with the best information available, gathered not only from individual scientists but from many organizations as well.

In order to give this kind of help more quickly, FAO has established regional offices in various parts of the world to which those near by may turn — in Rome, Italy, for Europe; in Cairo, Egypt, for the Middle East; in Bangkok, Thailand (Siam), for Asia and the Far East.

Many of the questions which come to FAO are about seeds, especially the new varieties that plant breeders have produced after long and patient work. Every 4-H Club member who plants corn knows about hybrid corn which grows sturdily in all kinds of weather and is not so seriously harmed by insect pests as are other varieties. When 4-H's plant hybrid corn, they get more of it on every acre and it is better corn, too. Rust-resistant wheat, beans without strings, strawberries twice the size of those our grandfathers ate — these are but a few of the things the new seeds are giving us today.

But there are plant scientists in every country. Today, through FAO, word about what they are doing is quickly reaching many countries. Seeds have always been great travelers. Centuries ago Arab traders picked up oranges in China and took them to the Middle East, the first stretch of their long journey. Rubber plants went by sailing vessel from Brazil to Ceylon, Malaya, and the East Indies. Potatoes, tomatoes, and tobacco left America for distant lands. Now seeds are traveling as never before. Sent by FAO, they are even going by airplane to experimental farms and laboratories of many countries, where they are tested for the different climates and used in new cross-breeding.

It is always fascinating to get the latest seed catalogues, right after Christmas, and go over the lists of vegetables and flowers, some of them new varieties, that may be planted in next summer's gardens. FAO is making a new kind of catalogue for the plant breeders of the world which one of them has called a dream come true. It is *The FAO Catalogue of Genetic Stocks,* which, when completed, will list all varieties of important food plants wherever they grow. With each plant there is to be full information about it, its strong points and its weaknesses and where it may be obtained. Now information is being collected on the world's two most important food crops, wheat and rice, and an amazing amount of data on the different varieties has already been sent out to plant breeders far and wide.

The governments of many countries are making this remarkable catalogue possible. The United States Department of Agriculture, which for many years has had its plant explorers and its splendid collections of stock plants, has placed its experience and knowledge at the service of FAO. The British Commonwealth, with its large collections of potato, cotton, and other plants, has done the same. So, too, the hundreds of government and plant breeding stations in the countries of the other member nations.

And the nations get back more than they give. Through FAO the United States already has received very welcome new plants — a bell pepper that resists disease; a muskmelon that matures early — a vital consideration in certain parts of our country. This pepper and this muskmelon came from China. From Japan, American farmers now have a sweet potato that grows better than other kinds and has a higher starch content. From Thailand has come a kind of apricot which is not harmed by early frost. And so it goes. FAO has set up the markers for a two-way traffic in seeds and plants.

But FAO's Secretariat does not stop at gathering information and writing letters. Like the county agents of the 4-H Clubs, its scientists go out to its members with their Know-How and their ability to Show-How. Teams are constantly leaving FAO headquarters for countries that have asked for help on some special problem. When they arrive, they enter into the same kind of partnership as UNICEF. FAO provides specialists to give their technical assistance. The government pays the expenses of the FAO team while it is at work and supplies its own team-member specialists. Often the FAO-government team trains new workers so that they may carry on after the special task is completed for which FAO has come.

Together the FAO-government partners discuss just who shall be chosen to go abroad to study on FAO fellowships. Returning, the fellows

FAO IS BRINGING SIAM
FISHERMEN MORE EFFICIENT
GEAR THAN THESE PRIMITIVE
BAMBOO POLES AND TRAPS

CHINESE FARM CHILDREN
WAITING PATIENTLY TO HAVE
THEIR CHICKENS VACCINATED
AGAINST NEWCASTLE DISEASE
WITH FAO-PRODUCED VACCINE

"THE RIGHT HOES
AND THE 'SHOW-HOW'
MUST COME FIRST,"
SAID NORRIS E. DODD
OF THESE BOYS IN THE
RICE FIELDS OF ASIA

bring back the new knowledge they have gained, and are of greater usefulness as they help their own people to help themselves.

What do the FAO-government teams do? Work as varied as that on any farm. FAO experts arrive in Italy to help with the blight that is attacking her chestnut trees, cutting down on Italy's food supply and her exports, for chestnuts are an important export. Before the FAO team members leave, they arrange for varieties of blight-resistant chestnut trees to be sent from China to Italy's experiment station. FAO's experts, going to Poland to work with its specialists in combating TB and other diseases in cattle, have sent in a supply of the new vaccines that will make the cattle immune to these diseases in the future.

"Rats and other pests are destroying huge amounts of our stored grain," writes Egypt. "Please help us." The suggestions FAO's team members make there come from the effective work of others in their parts of the world, where they have had the same trouble. An FAO expert goes to Austria to demonstrate the proper use of farm machinery. Specialists in fisheries go to Thailand to survey its fisheries and help draw up a plan for developing them. These are only a few of the many calls answered by FAO.

In addition to giving help to the member governments on single problems, FAO, the "county agent," often goes out to work with them in drawing up blueprints for the future for all phases of their agricultural activity. Such a mission spent two months in Nicaragua with the FAO-government partners working out a program for better plant production, forestry, and livestock breeding and production. In Bolivia the blueprint was for soil analysis, irrigation and drainage, forestry, and the cultivation of tropical crops. And so on and on. One of the largest of these missions has been that to Greece, where the partners made plans for the next twenty-five years and where the Greek people have already made an excellent start on those plans.

The book which FAO published about the work of this mission, *Report of the FAO Mission for Greece,* gives a good idea of just what a United Nations mission of any kind essentially is, for all missions proceed in the same general way. Like the fellowships, missions are an important part of the work of all the United Nations. "An FAO mission is a group of experts, usually drawn from several countries, which goes to a country or a region to study at first hand a given problem or group of problems related to food, agriculture, forestry, or fisheries. On the basis of this study it makes recommendations for action by the government or governments concerned. Recommendations may also be made for action by FAO and other international organizations.

"No mission is sent to any country except on request of its government and after determination by the Director-General of FAO that it is feasible and worth while."

"Region" is mentioned in this description because farmers' work and farmers' problems have no national boundaries. Just as the 4-H agriculturalists discovered, when they were in Washington, that no matter where they lived, they were facing the same needs and that it helped to exchange information on what they were doing, so it is with all agriculturalists. FAO therefore calls them together in groups of countries that are faced with the same problems.

More food for youth, for all the people of the world — and there can be if insect pests can be controlled. In a Latin-American regional conference, held at Tapachula, Mexico, FAO met with specialists from six Central American countries to discuss with them practical measures to be taken in the control of the locust. Since then eighteen South and Central American countries have joined in a regional campaign not only against the locust but also against other insect pests that are damaging their crops. This campaign is going on today and will continue. Shoulder to shoulder, the agriculturalists of these nations are working together.

More food — and there can be if the good earth, the soil, is taken care of. At FAO's soil-conservation conference in Italy specialists from seven countries in Europe and the Middle East met together to make their own kinds of plan.

More food — and there can be if, from the water that covers three fifths of the globe, more fish, so valuable to growing young people and children because of its animal protein, can be caught. Fishermen, "farmers of the sea" as FAO calls them, have done very effective work in the Atlantic Ocean. Comparatively the others of the Seven Seas have been very sketchily "farmed." Since 1902 the International Council for the Exploration of the Sea has been splendidly active. In 1948 FAO joined with its members and other ocean explorers to carry on joint research.

As a result, the great Indo-Pacific Fisheries Council was organized. Meeting for the first time in Singapore in March 1949, the delegates talked as fishermen do when they get together — about the best kinds of gear and equipment, where the fish are, what kinds they are, just how to catch them. In addition, they made lists of commercially important fish. They arranged for new maps to be made showing where the fish migrate in the Indo-Pacific area. They collected information about the ships of the various countries that could be used for fisheries research there, including commercial as well as naval vessels.

All felt it very appropriate that the head of FAO's Fisheries Division is named Finn, Dr. Donovan J. Finn. When Dr. Finn attended the second meeting of the Council, he also visited Lebanon, Egypt, Pakistan, Ceylon, Thailand, India, and the Philippines to talk over the help FAO could give to their fisheries and fishermen.

More food — and there can be if the diseases that attack animals are controlled. At Nairobi, Kenya, in Africa, delegates from countries through-out Asia and Africa met to discuss the problem of rinderpest, which is so deadly to cattle in that part of the world. The new vaccine against rinderpest, which FAO helped to develop, was demonstrated. And the reports that have since come in to FAO headquarters have told of its successful use in other countries, too.

More food — experts say that all the sugar consumed in the sweet-toothed United States could be produced from the forests and mill wastes of the United States Pacific Northwest area alone. More forestry products of all kinds are the concern of such FAO-inspired regional organizations as the European Forestry and Forestry Products Commission, whose members include forestry organizations from many countries there and individual lumber specialists. FAO called the first Latin-American Conference on Forestry, as well as the International Forestry and Timber Utilization Conference at Mysore, India.

More food — one of FAO's largest regional projects has been with rice. To half of the young people of the world, half the children, as well as half the adults — chiefly in Asia — rice is the most important food. In China, when a man is well paid and does little work, in other words has a soft job, he is known as a "rice barrel," meaning that he is good for nothing except storage. If a man is looking for a job, he is said to be "looking for a rice bowl," and if he gets a good one, he has "a good rice bowl."

At FAO's invitation, in 1949, the governments of the great rice-growing countries joined together in the International Rice Commission, the first time that an international organization to increase and improve production of one of the world's most important foods has been formed. The Commission's first meeting was held in Thailand, at Chulalongkorn University in Bangkok. At this meeting the idea for a catalogue of genetic stocks for rice was discussed enthusiastically. Fertilizing also was taken up, as well as crop rotation, irrigation, storage, marketing, and the many other things vital to those who grow rice.

But plans made must be carried out, and many more experts are needed to do so. In Lahore, Pakistan, a three-month training course was opened late in 1950 for government agricultural officials in Asia and the Far East. This was made possible by a special partnership, the United Nations and the Economic Commission for Asia and the Far East working with FAO and the International Bank for Reconstruction and Development. The courses given were on the preparation of new large-scale agricultural and industrial projects and their presentation to national and international lending institutions in such a way that they make good financial sense.

More food — yes, but something else must be thought of, too. Your mother, marketing for your family's meals, knows that the kinds of food to buy are just as important as the amount. For you must have the balance that will give you the proteins, the starches, the minerals, and the vitamins that will make your body strong. FAO's nutritionists are thinking of this same thing and are working with the various governments to encourage their people not only to grow more food but to plant the right variety — something they have perhaps not done before.

José Santos and his two best friends in the Mathematical School in Pangasinan in the Philippines have special reason for being grateful to UN's nutritionists, for through them the three boys were cured of night blindness.

This is how it happened. When the UNICEF field workers went to the Philippines and gave physical examinations to the young people and children, they discovered that most Filipino diets were lacking in certain important vitamins. Since it was entirely possible for the people in the Philippines to grow the vegetables and other foods that would bring the needed vitamins, the UNICEF-government partners, in co-operation with FAO, decided to have School Feeding Demonstration Centers. In these centers school lunches would be served that would give children and young people the food values they needed. UNICEF, then, provided the milk, the meat, the cod-liver oil and fats, and the Philippine Government members of the team saw to it that there were green and yellow vegetables, other vegetables and fruit, fish, beans or peanuts, and rice.

These lunches, served to José and his friends each school day at the Mathematical School, cured them. For a long time they had been able to see only by daylight and had had to leave school early in order to find their way home. Within a short while after the lunches started, the sight of all three was almost normal.

Wherever the school lunches were served, parents, public health workers, doctors, nurses, and teachers were invited to come to see for themselves how much the health of the boys and girls was improving. To show just what could be raised in home and other gardens, more than a thousand boys and girls in Manila had vegetable plots as part of their schoolwork, and the vegetables they grew were cooked for the school lunches.

Then Mrs. Dulce L. Bocobo, a citizen of the Philippines and Nutrition Officer for FAO, joined the UN team to make a study of undernourished young people and children from the time they started eating the UNICEF-government meals. Making her physical examinations and her research at the Institute of Nutrition in the Philippine General Hospital in Manila, Mrs. Bocobo added to the government's knowledge of certain native food plants that can well be included in Filipino meals.

When Andromache Tsongas became FAO Nutritionist in Greece, it was a group of young girls who gave her some of her best help. Born in Greece, Miss Tsongas received her nutrition training in Boston. When she returned to Greece, the FAO-government partners asked her to work out plans for interesting the Greek people in raising new kinds of crops which would bring them needed food values. One of these foods was potatoes, and Miss Tsongas and her associates worked hard to interest the Greek people in planting and eating more of them.

When UNICEF went to Greece, Miss Tsongas was appointed a representative on its team. "Our UNICEF team specialized on breakfast," Miss Tsongas said later in a UN radio interview. "You see, in Greece it is not customary to eat much, if any, breakfast. But the children needed it. So we decided to serve breakfast to them each school day — a cup of milk, a roll made of whole-wheat flour, some fat, and some raisins. This would be good for them and then maybe their breakfast habit would become so well established that the next generation would eat breakfast.

"UNICEF provided the milk and the fat. The Greek Government furnished the raisins and the rolls, which were baked in village or town bakeries. We made quite a point of the milk, for many mothers in Greece hadn't known what a valuable food milk is for their children. Skim-milk powder was entirely new to them. I should point out that this situation has been true of mothers in other of the countries where UNICEF has gone, not alone in Greece. But having seen what milk can do, today thousands of mothers have taken up the cause of larger milk production in the places where they live, with the result that many more children are now drinking milk.

"I had seven young girls, home economics students, going out under my direction to teach mothers about milk, especially dried skim milk. They went from village to village, talking to the various women's groups, visiting the schools, checking with the teachers, the village priests, the presidents of the communities, and so on. I can't honestly tell you that every mother who heard them was convinced. But a great many were. Yes, my girls did a splendid job."

Before Miss Tsongas went to Greece, before the work of the UN partners, the Greek Government did not have a nutrition service. Today there is a law requiring it. And Andromache Tsongas, FAO Nutritionist, is working with the government to carry out that law.

More food — such is FAO's work to help produce it. Has FAO been successful in its aim? Norris E. Dodd answered this question in *The United Nations Bulletin* in 1949. Mr. Dodd, successor to Sir John Boyd Orr as FAO's Director-General, is an outstanding Oregon farmer. Starting years ago with only a few acres of uncleared land, he has built up a farm of two thousand acres, fully mechanized with the most modern equipment, where he grows wheat and barley and raises Hereford beef cattle. Mr. Dodd in himself exemplifies FAO's Know-How and ability to Show-How.

His *Bulletin* article was called "The Turning Point in the World Food Situation." He said: "Since World War II, the better-fed countries have surpassed their pre-war production per person so that they are better fed than ever before. But in countries that were ill fed before the war, for the most part the people are worse off than they were before."

Why is this? Because there are more babies and small children than ever in the ill-fed countries. Because the population has increased faster than the production of food, which has always been inadequate. Because these are the underdeveloped countries of the world, where the people are poor, undernourished, uneducated, unable to help themselves unless they are given a start.

It was of them that President Truman was thinking when he said to Congress: "Greater production is the key to prosperity and peace. And the key to greater production is a wider and more vigorous application of modern scientific and technical knowledge."

In 1950 the member countries of the United Nations and the Specialized Agencies voted more than twenty million dollars to help the peoples of the under-developed areas of the world in their upward climb. To this large fund each of the member nations, including the United States, has contributed its share. It is a tribute to the technical assistance so ably rendered by FAO in its early years of existence that when this technical assistance fund was divided up, FAO was to receive twenty-nine per cent of the total amount. WHO and UNESCO, together with other parts of the UN, also received financial recognition from the fund.

When Norris E. Dodd took a trip around the world, at every stop he went out onto the farms to talk with the farmers. He told about these visits when he came back, over the UN radio and in an article "Hoes and 'Show-How' Come First," in *The New York Times Magazine*. "Where most of the rice of the world is raised, it's all an operation by hand," he said. "The rice farmer sets out a little plot of rice. Then he transplants all those plants, one at a time, by hand. Backbreaking labor — cruel labor. Then he irrigates that and weeds it by hand. Then he cuts it with a sickle. If you'd give him a scythe so that he could stand up and cut instead of kneeling over to cut it with a sickle, you'd bring him ahead many, many years. Then the rice is carried into his quarters and threshed by hand with a flail or by animals and people walking around it.

"I saw a dozen boys in a class, down on their knees, learning to hoe with short-handled hoes. There are plenty of places, remember, where just a good hoe is an advanced agricultural implement. One of those boys with a common ten-dollar hand cultivator or wheel hoe could have done the job better and how I did want to give them all that cultivator, that hoe!

"Perhaps you will say that since there is nothing else for the boys to do, where people are already so crowded on the land, they might as well be doing things the hard way. Or perhaps you are of the other extreme school and will say, why not train them to be tractor mechanics? But there are no tractors for them to drive, and there can't be for a long time. Still, I don't see any percentage in inefficient methods when just a little improvement could make so much difference."

When the FAO-government partners come to these people, are they interested in changing their primitive ways? "In one village in India," continued Mr. Dodd, "I talked with a farmer who stood with one hand proudly on the head of his little daughter, just as farmers will stand and talk with a visitor anywhere in the world. He was especially proud because that nine-year-old daughter was the 'official reader,' the only person in the village who could read.

" 'I hope she won't have to do like her mother,' he told me. Her mother had gone to work in the fields when she was the daughter's age. Where one person's labor just about feeds one person, schooling time is a handicap to the family, a thing to be grudged."

So it is that FAO's special task in the days immediately ahead will be for the young people, the children, their families, and older friends who have never yet had enough to eat.

Speaking in New York City, Gove Hambridge, adviser to FAO's Director-General, said: "In a Latin-American country a few days ago I talked to a small group of poor Indians living on their community lands. These Indians were growing a crop of summer wheat. They had not been able to grow summer wheat in that countryside before. But now they had seed of new disease-resistant varieties, developed through international co-operation in research.

"On these same farms I saw water brought for the first time by irrigation pumps onto the dry, parched land. Never before could the people there get more than three crops in some seven years. Now they can grow food every year.

"These simple things are giving these people new life and new hope. I saw this in their eyes. I heard it on their lips. And I knew that what I saw, what I heard, was a symbol of the whole aspiration of FAO."

Let there be bread.

A C-47 TB PLANE LEAVES COPENHAGEN
WITH MEDICAL SUPPLIES
FOR THE YOUNG PEOPLE AND CHILDREN
OF THIRTEEN EUROPEAN COUNTRIES

HERE IN THE CARRARA, ITALY, HOSPITAL,
STREPTOMYCIN CURED FOURTEEN-YEAR-OLD
MARIUCCIA STOPEDAN
OF TUBERCULOUS MENINGITIS

POLISH CHILDREN WAIT
OUTSIDE THEIR SCHOOL FOR THEIR
ANTI-TUBERCULOSIS VACCINATION

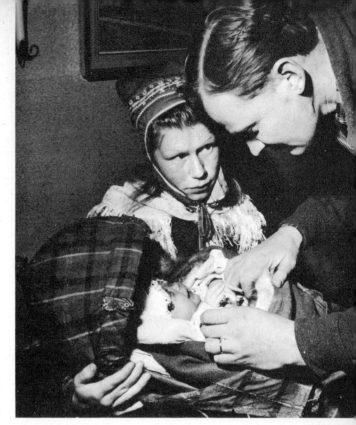

"IS HE ALL RIGHT?"
A YOUNG ROUVANIEMI, LAPLAND,
MOTHER ASKS HER DOCTOR, BACK
FROM PARIS MEDICAL TRAINING

ON CALL
DAY AND NIGHT

Abed and Nasir always went home from school the same roundabout way, which included one full stop. Going down into the business district of Cairo, they hurried past the tall buildings and shops, pushed through the crowds at the markets, until they came to the sightseeing headquarters. That was the full stop. No matter when they arrived, a car was sure to drive up within a short time to let out tourists who had been to Gizeh to see the Pyramids.

Such curious people! The chauffeurs never failed to have stories about the strange things the visitors said and did. How some, insisting upon scrambling all the way to the top of a pyramid, would turn right around and go back with scarcely a glance down below. And what they paid to have their pictures taken sitting on a camel! They didn't seem to mind having spent the money, though. They were always laughing and joking when they came back.

But one October day in 1947 there was no laughter or gaiety among them as they alighted from the car. Some, looking very pale, walked away quickly. Others, who lingered, talked in low, frightened voices. What had happened? Abed and Nasir ran over to Kassem, who was still sitting in the driver's seat, counting his tickets.

"Did one of the visitors fall from a pyramid, perhaps, and bounce?" asked Abed. And Nasir laughed loudly over his friend's wit.

"Laugh while yet you may," replied Kassem, looking up ominously from his tickets. "For soon you will be dead. I, too. All, all will be dead."

The boys stared. This from Kassem, jolliest chauffeur of them all. "What is ——" began Abed.

"What, indeed?" interrupted Kassem. "It has come again. A man driving through Gizeh said it. That of which my grandfather has told many times — the cholera. Over forty years ago it came, spreading like wildfire. None escaped. All died. My grandfather saw it."

Then, throwing the tickets down upon the seat, he sprang from the car and shouted, "Run! Run for your lives!" And suited his action to his words.

The boys ran, frenziedly pushing their way through the crowds, dodging automobiles, separating as they neared their homes. Dashing around a corner, Abed collided with a young man whose armful of books flew to the ground.

"Fool!" cried the young man. Then, "Abed! Stop! Stop at once and pick up my books!"

Abed skidded to a stop. It was his brother, Orah, on his way home from the American University of Cairo where he was studying law so that he might join their father in his practice.

Abed clutched Orah's arm. "We are going to die," he gasped. "You, our mother, our father — all of us."

Orah frowned. "Have your wits forsaken you?"

"It is the cholera. It has come. A man driving through Gizeh told Kassem."

"Kassem's head has caught fire from the sun thus to believe a passer-by," declared Orah.

"It is true. I know it," insisted Abed. "Quick, we must run. It spreads like wildfire. Kassem said it."

"Calm yourself, my brother," said Orah sternly. "Now then, pick up the books. Then we shall go home and there telephone Allee at his hospital. He is more to be relied upon than some stranger." Allee was their cousin, an interne in Cairo's largest hospital.

"How is it that Kassem is certain all will die?" Orah asked as they hastened on.

"His grandfather saw the cholera when it came before. All died. None escaped."

Orah laughed scornfully. "How is it, then that Kassem's grandfather lives to tell it?"

"Oh," said Abed.

The operator at the hospital who answered Orah's call was brusque and sharp. "Allee cannot possibly come to the phone. Who are you? Where are you?"

"I am his cousin," replied Orah. "And I am in my own home."

"Then stay there. Do not leave. The radio will tell you what you are to do. The cholera has come."

Before night the government of Egypt had closed all markets, fairs, and other gathering places. Strict guard had been set up at the borders. No one except officials was to go out or to come in. Doctors, nurses, Red Cross workers were on their way to the place where the cholera had broken out. And the radio had informed Abed's family that they must remain at home until they could all be vaccinated.

For what Kassem had said was true. Cholera does spread like wildfire. Five times during the last century it has raced across Europe, three times jumping the Atlantic to North America.

Even before their government had sent out its warnings to the Egyptian people that October day in 1947, notification of the outbreak had gone from Cairo to the Epidemic Control Station of the United Nations' World Health Organization in Geneva. From Geneva warning at once sped throughout Europe. Throughout the Americas, by way of the Pan American Sanitary Bureau in Washington. Throughout the Indian Ocean and Pacific areas, via Singapore. And from Alexandria for Africa, the Middle East, and the Mediterranean region. Warning around the world. At seaports and airports inspectors were alerted.

And the peoples of the world went into action. Serum for the vaccination of all the Egyptian people must be sent at once. But there were nineteen million Egyptians. Would there be enough serum in even all the countries combined? There would. In the United States all vaccine laboratories dropped everything else to concentrate on making anti-cholera serum. Epidemic specialists, including Red Cross workers, were called out and within forty-eight hours were on their way to Egypt, each plane loaded with as much serum as it could carry. Planes were also on their way from Afghanistan, Australia, Belgium. From Brazil, China, Italy, the Netherlands. From Spain, Turkey, the U.S.S.R. From the Union of South Africa, Japan, Korea. From the International Red Cross. In all, more than thirty-two tons of anti-cholera vaccine, blood plasma, and other urgently needed supplies were shipped.

For four weeks the epidemic grew, spreading throughout Egypt. But by the first week in December it had been virtually stopped — the shortest time in history that so great an epidemic has been checked so quickly. In addition, the number of deaths was drastically cut down — from eighty-five per cent in the cholera epidemic of forty-five years before which Kassem's grandfather had experienced to but little more than forty-eight per cent.

The peoples of the world could act together swiftly because the World Health Organization of the United Nations was ready. When WHO was established, in 1946, one of its first projects was the organization of wider epidemic control. Taking over what had been developed under the League of Nations, WHO decided to use telegraph and radio more widely and to extend the stations to which emergency messages should go. A committee of experts also drew up for all countries a list of preventive sanitary measures and the most up-to-date treatment not only for cholera but for smallpox, plague, typhus, yellow fever, and other of the fast-spreading diseases.

Today, twice a day messages go out from ten powerful transmitters near Geneva to all parts of the world, rerouting the reports steadily received there from all continents.

"Typhus in Afghanistan." The warning to all. Airplanes loaded and sped on their way. Then — "Everything under control."

"Yellow fever in Bolivia." Under control with WHO working through the Pan American Sanitary Bureau.

"Smallpox has broken out in South Africa." A WHO expert arrives to help combat it. Under control.

Such were the messages, such the emergency help extended by WHO during its first three years. Such is the work that has continued, that will continue, that has been called by those of the medical profession one of the great achievements of our time. No matter where a person lives, WHO's epidemic-control protection reaches out to him.

Being able to act swiftly in case of epidemics, important though that is, was but one part of what the nations of the world had in mind when, after signing the United Nations Charter in San Francisco, they took steps to establish a UN organization which would work for a healthier and therefore a happier world. They called it the World Health Organization, and by the middle of the year 1950, seventy-four nations had signed WHO's constitution, united in their belief that: "The highest attainable standard of health is one of the fundamental rights of every human being, and is fundamental to the attainment of peace and security." Health itself, according to WHO's constitution, is "complete physical, mental, and social well-being, and not merely the absence of disease and infirmity."

Better health for all — this great goal is never forgotten by WHO's World Health Assembly as the delegates from its member nations meet annually to review progress and vote on new plans. It is never forgotten by its executive board of eighteen members from eighteen different countries when they come together several times each year. Nor does WHO's Director-General forget it. The first Director-General, chosen to administer WHO's work for five years, was the famous Dr. Brock Chisholm of Canada whose valuable and distinguished experience includes executive medical work for the Canadian Government and Army as well as long and successful private practice.

Just as the Public Health Service of the United States Government is always on the alert for what will bring better health to the citizens of the United States, so WHO thinks of and acts for people around the world. Its Secretariat at WHO's headquarters in Geneva includes medical experts who have many different kinds of special knowledge and who are continuously on call to use that knowledge for the governments that ask for it. Those in WHO's field offices are also on call — in New Delhi, India, for southeast Asia; in Alexandria, Egypt, for the eastern Mediterranean area; in Washington, D.C., for the Americas; and elsewhere.

And WHO is on call for the United Nations itself to give technical assistance such as that rendered UNICEF in its emergency food work and its BCG campaigns. WHO and UNICEF are close partners in many ways. WHO experts advise on UNICEF's health projects for young people and children. Money from the Fund has made possible special work for youth in various countries where the WHO-government teams are at work.

FAO is another active WHO partner. Together they develop nutrition projects. WHO consults FAO on its anti-malaria campaigns and other plans — which is to be expected, for food and health are inseparable. With UNESCO, WHO has worked out a very interesting plan for the field of medical science. For a long time there have been many medical-science organizations around the world which have done much splendid work. Through UNESCO and WHO they have now been brought together "to foster international understanding in the field of medical sciences." When they met in Brussels to form a mutual organization, forty of them were represented, by delegates who came from five continents. Through this "Congress of Medical Science Congresses," as it has been called, that mutual understanding has already grown. And as they meet together in the future, those in each will come to know more about what the others are doing, and duplication of work will be lessened.

WHO's Geneva headquarters is a very busy place. There the Secretariat handles the hundreds of letters that arrive every year asking for advice. With the carefully given answers, medical literature is often sent, including WHO's own bulletins. Calls for help out in the field are also considered at Geneva and decisions are made as to just where WHO's experts shall go.

Out from Geneva, too, WHO sends its own calls, inviting experts from around the world to meet there and pool their knowledge for the benefit of people everywhere. From their own countries, often far distant, the specialists come together. One such meeting was to discuss the best ways to cure mumps, measles, chicken pox, and other so-called diseases of childhood. And after the discussions were over, WHO sent out bulletins to its member countries telling them about the conclusions the specialists had reached. Many doctors thus benefited — and their young patients benefited, too.

When a group of executive nurses from many countries met in Geneva, on WHO's call, they talked about what the best kind of nurses' training is, about how the nursing profession may be made more attractive to young people as well as more effective. And again the bulletins went out.

For one plan on which WHO is working a number of meetings have already been held and many more will be. That plan is for the standardization of drugs. Have you ever thought how convenient it is, and how important to your health, no matter where you travel in the United States, to be able to buy in any drugstore the same kind of medicine that you get at

WHEN ECUADOR'S EARTHQUAKE
MADE THOUSANDS HOMELESS,
ALL THE UNITED NATIONS
GAVE DISASTER HELP

THE JAM
THAT TASTED
SO DELICIOUS
TO THESE
BULGARIAN
SCHOOLGIRLS
CAME FROM
URUGUAY

IN TERAI, INDIA,
AN ANTI-MALARIA WHO TEAM
SPRAYS THATCHED ROOFS
WITH DDT, TO KILL
GERM-CARRYING MOSQUITOES

home? If you happen to need soda bicarbonate, you can rely on any standard brand. When the tablets in the bottle are labeled "five grains," you know what that means.

WHO is working for this same kind of drug standardization around the world. Years ago the League of Nations started upon it because it was greatly needed even then. Today that need is greater than ever before. Hospitals, doctors, health workers in all countries need it. Travelers, boarding airplanes for distant places, need it. However, before the plan can be put into universal practice many agreements must be worked out between countries, and that will take time. But WHO is looking ahead and has already made progress.

The calls that come to WHO in Geneva for help to be given in the member countries are of many kinds. Singly, or in teams and missions, the experts set out to answer them. Some calls are for the making of country-wide health surveys, so that the governments' ministries of health may have carefully made plans of action. And the teams leave to serve as did one in Ireland. There, joining with the Irish experts, the WHO-government partners traveled about the country, making a study of what Irish health workers were already doing and what they needed. In the plan they worked out, the health of Irish young people and children had a prominent place.

One of the largest of these survey missions sent out by WHO during its first years was that to Italy, in which the Rockefeller Foundation joined WHO and the Italian Government. The health plan they made was for a long period of years, and it covers as many kinds of health activity as the United States Public Health Service works upon. Already the Italian Government has carried out various parts of it, including the establishing of a national nutrition center.

Member countries that for years have been doing excellent health work look to WHO for a checkup. When Dr. Leonard A. Scheele, Surgeon General of the United States Public Health Service, attended the meetings of WHO's World Health Assembly in Rome, he was so impressed by the expert knowledge of J. C. Dawes, mechanical engineer of the British Ministry of Health, he asked WHO to send Mr. Dawes to this country for a sanitation survey.

It was arranged, and Mr. Dawes spent two months in the United States, traveling from coast to coast, visiting twenty-one large cities as well as smaller towns and rural communities. The report he then wrote, *The Storage,*

Collection and Disposal of Domestic Refuse (including Garbage) in the U. S. A., has been of great help to our public-health officials. Available to all of them, it is full of practical suggestions. What did Mr. Dawes find? The good and the bad.

"This report is an example of how valuable the experts of the United Nations are to every member country," Dr. Scheele has said.

Some of the calls arriving in Geneva are for WHO experts to come and help train medical workers, and the teams leave for that. In Ethiopia, where hospital assistants and sanitation workers were desperately needed, beginners' courses were started at once. Before the WHO members of the team left, there were one hundred and thirty graduates from these courses, and instructors had been trained to teach more.

When Dr. Leo Eloesser, a famous American chest specialist, retired as professor of Stanford University's Medical School, he joined WHO's large mission to China, later also working with UNICEF. In a province of North China, he conducted classes in surgery and public-health training. And he himself did his full share of the teaching.

Speaking to his students in what his friends called a "fantastic mixture of Chinese and English" (he never did learn even pidgin English), he nevertheless managed to make himself understood. "Carrying out health measures is simple," he told them. "You need not have studied medicine for six years in order to be able to kill lice; to dig a *muo-fang* [privy]; to boil your drinking water; to recognize a hookworm egg. These things are simple and very, very useful."

After he had been at work for some time Dr. Eloesser reported to WHO: "Most of the students have learned to do what they have been taught—simple sanitary measures such as how to detect defects in the water supply and to remedy the situation. How to destroy breeding places for mosquitoes, flies, and the like. They know the characteristics of the common infectious diseases, are able to vaccinate against typhoid and smallpox. They can give first aid, assist in childbirth. And they know how to win the co-operation of the people."

Did his students carry out his teaching when they returned to their homes? Well, there was Aunt Kuo. "Aunt Kuo" was what the other members of the class called her, for she came from Kuo Ta Niang, a village in Shuang-shu tsun, Tung Hsien, China. Aunt Kuo could not read or write, but for twelve out of her fifty-seven years she had been the one to whom all her village turned when babies were born. Although half the babies died, nevertheless the village continued to have faith in her.

When Aunt Kuo was chosen to attend a WHO course in Tung Hsien, she appeared promptly. The lessons were simple and Aunt Kuo understood them all. She learned she must cut her fingernails short before she helped with the birth of a baby. That she must wash her hands in hot, soapy water. That if she could possibly get it, she must use *shao chiu — spirits that burn*, alcohol — for sterilizing her instruments. If she could not get alcohol, she must boil the instruments for a long time in water. And never again, never, was she to roll newborn babies in sand as she had always done. Instead, she must bathe them with oil.

Bursting with zeal, Aunt Kuo went back to Kuo Ta Niang. First she sought out a friend who could read and write. "You are to put down what I say," she directed. "Leave nothing out. Then you can read it back to me if I forget."

With a gleam in her eye she next descended upon the women who were expecting babies. "You are to lie down and rest more," she commanded, then added the other instructions she had learned in her course. To those who demurred, she had her answer. Very well, they could get someone else. Meekly the rebels obeyed.

When, later, a WHO field worker visited Aunt Kuo to see how she was getting along, he found her boiling cloths and clothes in her homemade rice steamer. "Not one of my babies has died since I went to the school," she announced triumphantly. "Six have I had. All live."

Checking, the field worker found that Aunt Kuo had forgotten nothing. As for her calling them "my babies," who was he to say that they were not?

Such are the calls, such the work of WHO, day by day, week by week, month by month, year by year. To it all are added large and concentrated attacks on the diseases that are striking down the greatest number of people in the world. Which, in turn, means the greatest number of teen-agers and children. Malaria and tuberculosis are two of these diseases, and at its first World Health Assembly meeting, the delegates voted to work against them in the places where they are most widespread.

Thirteen-year-old Aleko in his village home in northern Greece knew nothing about this decision. Yet because of it he was to be freed from the fear that had haunted him since he was a very small boy. It was malaria that he feared and hated. And he hated the mosquitoes which he knew brought it. It had done no good to move the rice fields a mile and a half from the village. The mosquitoes came into their home just the same. Time and again his father had to stay away from the fields because he was sick with malaria. His mother, too, was often ill with it. And when she looked at Aleko, her eyes were anxious. How soon would he, too, be stricken?

In deciding to start its International Malaria Campaign in Greece, WHO did so for two reasons. The first was because Greece was one of the worst malarial trouble spots. For centuries the Anopheles mosquito, carrier of malaria, had been breeding in the swamps there, bringing untold misery to the Greek people. The second reason was because FAO's mission to Greece asked for WHO's help.

"We cannot hope for real progress in greater food production here in Greece," wrote one FAO worker, "while thousands of farmers are being kept from their work because of malaria."

To direct its malaria campaign in Greece, the WHO-Greek Government partners appointed Dr. James Vine of Australia, an expert in fighting epidemics, with Daniel E. Wright of the United States Health Service, one of the world's greatest malaria specialists, to act as his assistant. With them were eleven doctors, including Greek physicians, forty-nine medical officers, and two hundred and thirty-seven foremen of spraying teams. Local teams of Greek laborers were also recruited in those places where Greece's malarial swamps were located.

Hundreds of barrels of DDT were shipped in. With the DDT came portable sprayers, much like those for fighting forest fires, for use in spraying the homes. For spraying the swamps, eighteen old airplanes were fitted up with tanks in their rear cockpits and spray nozzles on their exhausts. Three Greek Royal Air pilots were sent to the United States to learn crop-dusting techniques, and when they returned, they trained others.

At length the WHO-government partners were ready. And the Greek people were ready, too. For months men and women had been going out among them — to Aleko and his parents and the others in their village — explaining what was to be done and why it was important to spray every nook and cranny of their homes with DDT.

To work, then, the malaria teams. Roaring low over the swamps, in one year the planes sprayed ninety-six thousand acres. In the same length of time other teams sprayed five thousand, seven hundred homes of three million, five hundred thousand Greek citizens. Then on, the next year, to more swamps, more homes.

Did it help? In two years the death rate from malaria in Greece dropped sharply, in some places from as much as eighty-five to five per cent. The anxiety was gone now from the eyes of Aleko's mother. Aleko had lost his fear. And he had more to eat because his father, no longer frequently sick, worked steadily in the fields. It was the same everywhere. In all, the Greek farmers raised almost half again as much in the hitherto stricken districts.

On the WHO malaria workers went, this time to India, a place decided upon with FAO for the next attack. Accompanying them were a number of the Greek experts who had requested service in other countries. Behind them were the teams of trained Greek workers who would continue to carry on. And the Greek Ministry of Health had an anti-malaria plan not only for the following year but for years to come. Yes, even on to the time when Aleko himself would be a farmer with a family of his own.

In answering the urgent call from India the WHO team members were aware of the difficulties. They knew that at least one hundred million people there were suffering from malaria, half of them young people and children. They knew about the jungles. They knew about the language difficulties, the many obscure dialects. But steadfastly they went ahead, knowing, too, that Indian doctors and other medical workers with fine training were waiting to join them in their work.

Head of the WHO team assigned to Terai was Dr. George Belios of Athens. When Dr. Belios returned to Geneva, he was interviewed for *Collier's* magazine by David Perlman, an American newspaperman. "I've never seen anything like Terai," Dr. Belios told Mr. Perlman. "Three hundred and fifty square miles of wet, smelly jungle with one dirt track running down the middle, impassable most of the time. Fifteen thousand inhabitants living in mud-walled, thatch-roofed villages, and every few years the entire population dying of malaria. Just imagine, two hundred and fifty-six tiny villages and every few years death emptying them all.

"With the British health nurse and the other members of our team we set up headquarters in a run-down sugar factory. And we had our labor troubles — tigers, panthers, and pythons roamed the factory grounds and scared away our Indian spraying squads.

"Tackling the villages took tact and patience. The local Buxa tribes are a matriarchal society, which means the women run the villages. And the women didn't want foreigners spraying strange chemicals over their kitchens and sleeping rooms. Tied in with their tribal religion is the custom of plastering cowdung on the walls of their homes. Each time that happened we had to go back and spray with our DDT again.

"Some villages were so inaccessible that it took our team seven hours of plodding through the mud to get there. And then we'd have to wait while the Buxa matriarchs rang bells and lighted lamps to propitiate their goddesses.

"It was hard to change those habits of centuries. But once we had done a few villages, the others came more easily. Word began to spread that where our sprayers had been at work the villagers were sleeping better at night; that the village cows, no longer eaten alive by flies, were giving more milk."

Dr. Belios left India because he was stricken with a baffling tropical disease for which his doctor associates could find no remedy. But although he knew his sickness might well prove fatal, he told Mr. Perlman, "Those months in India were worth while whether I ever work again or not. Even before I came away there hadn't been a single new case of malaria in any of our villages. Not a one."

Within three years and in similar ways WHO's malaria-control work was being carried on in other countries in Europe as well as in Greece, in other countries in Asia as well as in India, and in Latin America. To its attack on the Anopheles mosquito it added that on other insect health enemies. As its right-hand aide in many of these campaigns WHO has UNICEF. In certain places the insect-control campaign is planned for groups of countries, large regions where insects are especially harmful. Central America is one of these regions. There the WHO-UNICEF campaign in insect control is for the protection of two million people. WHO keeps in mind, too, airplanes and ships and railroad cars that go from country to country, advising on the best sprays to use and on the government controls to be set up against unwanted insect passengers. Effective insect control calls for constant watchfulness. One year's campaign must be followed by next year's steps to safeguard the gains made. And the WHO partners will do exactly that.

WHO's work against tuberculosis also reaches around the world. Many countries have asked WHO to make nationwide tuberculosis surveys and to give them suggestions on what they can do to prevent as well as cure this disease. Within three years the WHO team members went to countries in northern Africa, Asia, Europe, Latin America, and the Middle East. And it advised UNICEF on its BCG campaigns.

WHO calls meetings of experts to discuss new treatments being used with TB. When forty doctors from many countries met in Paris, the WHO-UNICEF conference was on streptomycin. All were agreed that in streptomycin potent help has at last been found for tuberculous meningitis, hitherto almost a hundred per cent fatal. The doctors reported on just how the new drug was being administered in their countries for this kind of TB. They discussed its use with other types of TB, its possibilities for yet other diseases.

The delegate from the United States to this conference was Dr. Edith Maas Lincoln, specialist on chest diseases of children at Bellevue Hospital, New York City, and a member of the faculty of the New York University Medical School. When she returned, Dr. Lincoln passed on to her fellow staff members in Bellevue what had been discussed in Paris and what she had learned there. And many other American doctors shared in the benefits of the conference through the articles by Dr. Lincoln that later appeared in medical publications.

When someone asked Dr. Lincoln just how the work of WHO differs from that of the international health and medical organizations which have been in existence for years and have done much excellent work, she replied: "WHO is different because it can act more quickly. And we need quick action today in order to know as soon as possible what can be done with the new drugs that are being discovered — to mention but one development of many."

One call comes from everywhere to WHO: "Help us to get more doctors, more nurses, more health workers of all kinds." For no country has enough. In some, half the population has only one doctor for every twelve thousand people.

In addition to the work of WHO's teams as they conduct training courses out in the field, WHO's fellowships are helping to meet this great need. Every year upward of four hundred men and women are chosen to study abroad on these fellowships. What each is to study is carefully decided upon by the WHO-government partners. It may be communicable diseases, public-health administration, maternal and child health, surgery, or any one of the other subjects in health education. Four hundred a year is not many in the face of the great need. But it is four hundred. It is four thousand in ten years, four thousand men and women returning to their countries to be of greater usefulness to their people.

And so the work of WHO goes on — and on.

Bulletin: WHO station wagon arrives in Ecuador, loaded with medical supplies for earthquake victims. Supplies include chemicals for purifying water, typhoid vaccine to prevent outbreak of epidemics. UNICEF jeeps bring DDT. WHO workers join with those of the government, FAO, UNICEF, the Red Cross, and other organizations in giving disaster help.

Bulletin: WHO sends expert to advise United Kingdom in large-scale attack against whooping cough.

Bulletin: WHO experts report experiments a success with mosquitoes captured at mosquito farm in Thailand. Now know how much DDT needed per square foot for anti-malaria campaign there.

Bulletin: WHO sends special serum to combat rabies among Iran's people bitten by wolves.

Bulletin: WHO announces establishment of World Influenza Center in London. Auxiliary centers for research already set up in twenty-seven countries including United States.

WHO — on call day and night. And as those calls are answered, everywhere the teamwork. Everywhere good friends made as those of many nationalities work together for a healthier, happier world.

It is all part of what Dr. Chisholm had in mind when he said: "It is recognized that a necessary part of the equipment of every human being is social health, the ability to live in harmony with other people of other kinds, with other traditions, with other religions, and with other social systems throughout the world."

SCHOOL, EVEN
ON HOT
DESERT SANDS,
WAS AN EVENT
TO THE YOUNG
PALESTINE
REFUGEES

THOUSANDS OF
MAKESHIFT SCHOOLS
WERE LIKE THIS
CROWDED ROOM
IN NESTORION,
GREECE, WHERE
A WAR-BLINDED BOY
PATIENTLY LEARNED
WHAT HE COULD

WITH THE SCHOOL
BOMBED OUT,
THIS HUNGARIAN
TEACHER
MET WITH
HIS STUDENTS
UNDER THE TREES

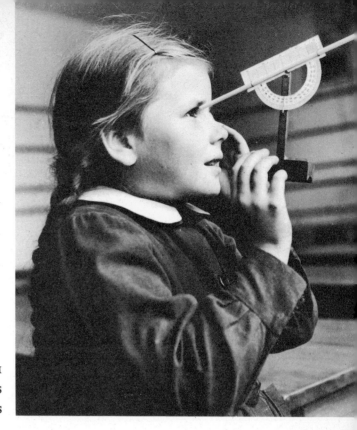

A STICK OF MACARONI
— AND THIS POLISH GIRL WAS
READY FOR HER SCIENCE CLASS

A BRIDGE
OF FRIENDSHIP
Sixteen-year-old Kyria crouched behind the bushes, peering at the children playing outside the ramshackle store building that was the school for all the boys and girls in the Greek village where she lived. Silly babies, she thought, trying to make a playhouse with those old bricks.

They certainly were stupid. And Kaity and the other girls who before the war had been her best friends were even more so. All they thought of nowadays was school. Evenings they sat at home, copying from the only book the Teacher had, so that next day they and the others would have something from which to study. What a way to spend your evenings!

It hadn't been like that during the war. Crawling right into the enemy's camp, she had stolen supplies from under their very noses. Not a week went by that she hadn't carried messages from one resistance group to another, playing deaf and dumb when she was caught, which wasn't often. Everybody had said then how wonderful she was. And when the war was over, she had been the one most praised of all the boys and girls.

But now! They praised everyone else. Never Kyria. Her mother scolded because she wouldn't go to this boring school that had no desks, no blackboard, no maps, no anything. If you could find a box, you sat on that. If you didn't have one, you plopped down on the floor. But that wasn't the worst of it. When she had tried going there for a couple of days, what had the Teacher done but put her in the arithmetic class with those not much more than infants. She had always been poor in arithmetic. Was it her fault, or wasn't it, that she was now further behind than ever? When those her age had been going to the secret classes held while the enemy was everywhere around, where had she been? Out running messages, that's where. It wasn't fair.

Kyria squirmed closer to the playing children. Brick by brick, they had managed to erect a foot or so of wall around a space for two rooms. Now they were leaving to get more bricks from the huge pile of rubble across the way. Kyria took a quick look about. Then, running low, she rushed to the wall and with well-aimed kicks wrecked what the children had done.

Back again under the bushes, she was triumphant. That would show them! When the brick-laden children returned, the scene was all she had hoped for. Furiously angry, some ran screaming indoors. Others stood numbly looking down at the wreck. When the Teacher and the older boys and girls came out, it was even better. They were indignant, bewildered. Who could possibly have done this without being seen? Kyria chuckled. She could do more than that!

Next day, Kyria was back under the bushes again. The children had started to rebuild their playhouse, but their hearts were not in it. Taking no pains to make the walls straight, listlessly they piled up the bricks every which way. One little boy wasn't working at all. Sitting on the ground away from the others, he watched them indifferently. He was Kosta, who lived with his mother's cousin because his father had been killed in the war and his mother had disappeared. How hard she, Kyria, had worked to find his mother! But although she had trekked miles, asking questions of everyone, she had come upon no trace of her.

Now Kosta began to sob, quietly, heartbrokenly. Into Kyria's mind flashed memory of him as he had been yesterday, so excited over the playhouse, so happily busy with the bricks. Next moment, Kosta felt gentle arms around him. Through his tears, he saw Kyria bending over him. Kyria, who of all the older boys and girls had done most for their village when the enemy was here. Not that he remembered it. It was just that the grownups were always telling stories about brave Kyria.

"Come, Kosta," Kyria was saying, "I will show you how to build your playhouse so that the walls won't fall down."

The other children came running. "Look," Kyria told them, "we'll use the side of the school for one of your walls. That will hold your playhouse up. Now then, bring over the bricks."

"Why the two rooms?" she asked as they rushed back and forth.

"Because, Kyria," Stelio, their energetic small leader, told her, "we need a kindergarten room for just us, nobody else, and we want one for the doctor." The seventy-six-year-old doctor, who lived two villages away, was their prime favorite.

"And we want some signs, Kyria," Stelio continued. "One that says 'Kindergarten' and one that says 'Doctor.' Will you help us make them?"

Signs! Where could she possibly find any paper? Or ink, or even a pencil, for that matter?

"I can lend a hand there," said a voice at Kyria's elbow. Kyria whirled around. The Teacher! Quickly she measured the distance to the bushes. If the Teacher tried to make her go into the school, she'd find out!

But the Teacher made no such suggestion. "That is a good idea," she said, "using the wall for one side of your playhouse. Wait here a minute, all of you. I'll be right out again." And she hurried back into the school.

When she returned, she was smiling. "Yes, there is just enough paper. I have been saving it for something special, and your playhouse is exactly that. Can you get hold of some soot this afternoon, do you think, Kyria? Mixed with water, it makes ink that will do, you know. And all of you children must look for more feathers for paintbrushes. We are almost out of them."

It wasn't much of a playhouse when it was finished. It had no roof, no doors. But the children loved its one room for just themselves, nobody else, and the other for their doctor friend who said it was exactly what he had been needing. And the signs! Fastened to the school wall, they could be read by everyone even though the letters were more than a little wobbly.

For three days after the playhouse was completed, Kyria was there at every recess time. On the fourth day it started to rain just as the children came running out. Rushing to take down the precious signs, they begged Kyria to come indoors with them. Surrounding her, determinedly they pushed and pulled until they got her to the door. Kyria looked inside suspiciously. Were the other girls going to laugh at her? They were not. With a casual hello, they went on with their own concerns. And the Teacher did nothing more than wave her hand. So Kyria stayed with the children, leaving as soon as recess was over.

Next day, the children had a new idea. Wouldn't Kyria be their teacher in the kindergarten room when it was sunny? They could bring their reading cards outdoors with them, the Teacher said. Kyria considered. Then, "All right," she told them.

The next thing that happened was the Teacher's saying, "You have done so well with the reading lessons, Kyria, why don't you try arithmetic? With so many to teach, I don't have much time for the babies."

Kyria flushed. Arithmetic!

"You can come a bit early before school starts each day, and I will go over the next lesson with you," the Teacher went on.

Suddenly Kyria laughed aloud. A teacher! That would show those snippy girls. Yes, she would do it. She would start tomorrow. She didn't think about rainy days. But by the time one came along, there she was inside the school — a teacher.

Several months later, after the others had gone home, Kyria stood beside the Teacher's box desk. Things were better now, there in their school. They had a blackboard and an eraser and some chalk. They had pencils and paper and a map. And they had ten books. Soon, the Teacher told them, they would have desks.

"I wish to thank you," Kyria said, "from the bottom of my heart."

The Teacher glanced down at the Honor Roll which she had announced a few moments before. Up near the top was Kyria's name, not among those of the small children but with those her own age.

"No need to thank me, Kyria. You did it yourself," the Teacher said.

"I was the one who kicked over the children's first playhouse," Kyria told her, relieved to admit it at last.

"I thought so."

"I hated everybody then," Kyria went on. "My mother, the other girls, you, every ——"

STARTING THE DAY AT CHORTIATIS, GREECE, WITH GYMNASTICS
IN FRONT OF THEIR OLD SCHOOL, PUPILS THEN GO TO CLASSES IN A NEAR-BY CHURCH

YUGOSLAV TEEN-AGERS
CONSTRUCTED CANALS, REGULATED RIVERS, REBUILT ROADS AND RAILROADS,
INCLUDING THIS TUZLA-BANOVIC LINE ON WHICH SIXTY-TWO THOUSAND WORKED

"No, not everybody," interrupted the Teacher. "You never stopped loving the children."

Then picking up a small booklet printed in English that Kyria had often noticed on her box desk, the Teacher fluttered its worn pages. "Listen to this, Kyria," she said. "You weren't the only one."

And translating into Greek as she went along, she read: "There is no doubt that many youths played an outstanding part in the war. They showed traits of endurance, daring, ingenuity and courage, imagination in their treks to discover lost parents, in their efforts to find food on which to survive, in assisting the resistance or underground movements. Today's world seems drab and unheroic to them."

Kyria listened, spellbound.

"One does not wonder that insubordination is rife," the Teacher continued, "disrespect evident, independence and arrogance offensively present. In many cases, these are the young people who were taught during the war to disobey the occupying authorities. Resistance was instilled in them. Sabotage and disobedience to authority were encouraged and lauded. They have been taught disobedience to authority and they are applying their learning."

Kyria, her eyes swimming with tears, choked, then said, "I was like that. I lied and I stole and I ——"

"Yes, all that," said the Teacher. "It is what war does to the young, Kyria. But never forget you loved the children."

"And now you are helping me so that I may learn to be a teacher like you. No, not like you, not that good. But a teacher."

"Not like me. Better," replied the Teacher softly. And arm in arm they walked from the school.

Behind them, the little booklet lay on the box desk. Under its cover picture of a group of boys and girls were the words: "Publication of UNESCO."

To give help to Kyria and the millions of other teen-agers, children, and their teachers in the war-devastated countries was among the first decisions made by UNESCO after it was founded as a Specialized Agency of the United Nations in 1946. The booklet that meant so much to Kyria's teacher, and therefore to her, was UNESCO's first expression of that help. It did not have many pages, that little booklet. The type in which it was printed was small, for every inch of paper was precious. Yet in the years ahead, it would always stand as a symbol of UNESCO's way of working.

In those days to come, UNESCO, the UN Educational, Scientific, and Cultural Organization, would call together large conferences of people from many countries — educators, scientists, writers, musicians, and others — to share their knowledge and experience with one another and to pass that knowledge, that experience on to the peoples of their countries. Missions would go out from UNESCO House, its world headquarters in Paris, to work with the governments so that there might be more and better schools, more libraries, more science laboratories — more of everything that gives youth wider opportunity to learn and to enjoy the beauty that creative artists have given the world.

This work of UNESCO would be of many kinds because its charter, soon to be signed by fifty-nine nation members, directed that it be so: "To contribute to peace and security by promoting collaboration among the nations through education, science, and culture, in order to further universal respect for justice, for the rule of law and for the human rights and fundamental freedoms which are affirmed for the peoples of the world." Ending with that phrase which resounds again and again in the United Nations, "Without distinction of race, sex, language, or religion."

Work of many kinds, yet all of it basically the same to the delegates to its General Conference meeting each year, to its executive board of eighteen members, to its Director-General and its Secretariat. For soon they would be saying that what UNESCO does is summed up in these six words: "The peoples speaking with the peoples," and in their speaking, coming ever closer together in understanding of one another.

The citizens of UNESCO's member countries would speak with one another, too, in their National Commissions, the "citizens' voice in UNESCO." In the United States this National Commission, under the Department of State, has one hundred members, including a representative chosen from the high school students of the country. With the educators, scientists, and other eminent citizens chosen for the Commission's membership, the high school representative has equal voice in the discussions and the voting.

Meeting for the first time under its Director-General, Julian Huxley, distinguished British scholar, the members of UNESCO's executive board started upon plans for their work. But for them, just as for FAO and WHO, there was one first urgent responsibility — those in the war-stricken countries. It was UNESCO's task to give help to schools like Kyria's, to the colleges, the universities, the scientific laboratories, the libraries, the museums destroyed by the war.

The governments in the stricken countries were already doing what they could for themselves, valiantly striving to carry out such plans for educational reconstruction as those made as far back as 1942, when, with bombs falling outside, the Allied Ministers of Education of the governments in exile had met in London under the auspices of the British Government. And side by side with their governments, the peoples themselves and their organizations were doing their best with their little. Already, too, help was arriving from those of other countries and their organizations. Yet that help was only the start. Everywhere the question was being asked: "Just what more is needed? Let us know."

UNESCO's executive board voted to help answer this question that was being asked by the generous people of the world. At once they would send missions to Austria, Belgium, Burma, China, Czechoslovakia, Ethiopia, France, Greece, Iran, Italy, Luxembourg, the Netherlands, the Philippines, Poland, and Yugoslavia. There the mission members would talk with the Ministries of Education and with the faculties of the schools, universities, and the rest, listing their needs. When the missions returned, UNESCO would send word far and wide of what they had seen and learned. Following them, other missions would be added, to Hungary, India, Malta, Singapore, North Borneo, and Sarawak, making twenty-one in all.

But it would take time for the missions to travel to the war-stricken countries, some of them so far distant. Today, this day, there were the thousands of teachers like Kyria's, struggling to keep their schools going with little or no equipment. Until the blackboards, the chalk, the paper, the pencils, and the rest could be sent them, they needed encouragement, needed the feeling that they were working with others. They needed, too, to exchange the ingenious ideas they were evolving. To some, for those "reading" classes with no books, the thought had occurred of inviting to their schools the old people of the neighborhood to tell the folk tales they knew so well and which were so priceless a part of their country's heritage. It was a plan that worked splendidly, yet many teachers had not thought of it. Some were using the teen-age rebels such as Kyria as assistants with the younger children.

But again, others had not thought of doing so. Even devices such as making ink from soot and water could helpfully be passed on.

In short, the teachers needed to get together. But how could they, when travel was impossible? UNESCO decided to bring them together in a booklet whose pages would be their meeting place. To collect the material for this booklet, it would send out a representative on a quick trip to talk with the teachers themselves, to see them with their boys and girls, and to get acquainted with the young people as well.

Since time was urgent, and since the teachers of Greece, one of the most severely devastated of all the stricken countries, were faced with every problem, every shortage that could be imagined, Greece was chosen as the one to be visited. And the Greek Government, from its limited resources, promptly donated the money for printing the booklet. Leonard S. Kenworthy, an American educator who was a member of UNESCO's Secretariat, was appointed to make the trip.

With Harold E. Snyder, director of the United States Commission on International Educational Reconstruction, Mr. Kenworthy flew to Athens. There a Greek interpreter joined them, and for three weeks they traveled about, going to Greek cities, towns, villages, and through the countryside, talking with groups of teachers and those alone in remote little schools.

Wherever they went, they found boys and girls excitedly eager for school. For every rebellious teen-ager such as Kyria, there were hundreds who were working sturdily to rebuild what had been destroyed. The teachers, too, were carrying on gallantly, with many clever makeshifts to show Mr. Kenworthy. Page after page of his notebook was soon filled with descriptions of these makeshifts. And on page after page he wrote down the questions the teachers asked him about how they could more wisely guide their young people and their children whose lives had been so shattered.

Back again at UNESCO House, Mr. Kenworthy set to work upon the booklet. Helping him were his Secretariat associates who had spent many years in the field of education. No detail jotted down in the notebooks was too small to be included. You need a large, bouncing ball for your small children's play hours? Make one with rags, stuffed with sawdust or anything else available. To be sure, such a ball will not bounce, but it will roll. And, "A non-bouncing ball is better than no ball at all." You have no blackboard?

Ask one of your neighbor painters to concoct something black and paint one of your walls with it. If you cannot do that, try this — and a variety of other suggestions for blackboard-making followed. Recipes for making chalk were put in. Ink from soot and water was there. And so on and on.

Next came the questions the anxious teachers had asked. "My children are restless, nervous, irritable. How can I help them overcome this?" "Many of my children are intolerant and prejudiced, especially toward those of other racial backgrounds. How can I best develop in them tolerance and understanding?" "Our children are hardened to the fact of death. How can we make them more sensitive to the importance and value of human life and personality?" It was the stark story of the terrible effects of war upon youth. And in writing their answers, Mr. Kenworthy and his associates turned for help to the wisdom in the books of the world's great educators.

What they wrote about the rebellious teen-agers such as Kyria was deeply understanding. "In all of the war-devastated countries there is a tremendous amount of physical reconstruction to be carried on. It has seemed advisable in some places to give groups of boys — and girls — responsibility for rebuilding a section of a town or certain buildings, so that they could feel this was their job, and that they would not be interfered with by adults and those 'in authority.' Such work can be rewarding when it is accompanied by some recreation and fun.

"Oftentimes this can be shared by boys and girls, the hard physical labor being done by the boys and the cooking of meals, the tending of smaller children in the community, and the preparation of materials for inside the new homes of community centers or schools being done by the girls.

"A youth council can also be set up within a village or city or rural area having, as its aim, aid of all kinds to young people. In its membership there should be a large percentage of young people and a sprinkling of understanding adults."

The booklet, called *The Teacher and the Post-War Child in War-Devastated Countries*, was written in English — since many could read that language — printed in record time, and sent out to the governments. It was distributed by them, not only to teachers like Kyria's but to those in large schools, in teachers' colleges, and in teachers' associations. In whole or in part, it was translated into other languages, including Czech, French, Hungarian, Swedish, and Dutch. Translated into German by arrangement with the Military Government educational officials, it was the first UNESCO publication to appear in Germany.

Many a struggling teacher, reading it, took heart in the thought of others meeting her same kind of problem, found courage that UNESCO was standing by to help her. And how welcome the concrete suggestions were! Soon word was arriving at UNESCO House of the ways in which they were being used. Many a tree is growing along European streets and roads today because of the booklet's story about the Dutch boys and girls.

"Partially because of lack of wood for fuel and partially because of a desire to destroy, buildings in the Netherlands were being torn apart and the wood smashed or carried away to be burned. In the Hague and elsewhere, a tree-planting campaign was started among school children to plant hundreds of trees in parks and along the streets, and it was soon discovered that these trees were not molested by the children, who seemed to take pride in their common endeavor."

So it was that the booklet became the symbol that it is — the peoples speaking with the peoples — teachers helping one another through UNESCO. In UNESCO's projects of the future this might be called technical assistance. But whatever the project, great or small, UNESCO's way of working would be the same.

By the time the booklet reached Kyria's teacher, the missions had begun returning to UNESCO House. All gave appalling accounts of the destruction done by the war to educational buildings and equipment. But they also brought stirring stories of the people's unconquerable spirit in every country visited.

"The best help you can give us," the Burmese Minister of Education had said, "is to help us help ourselves. We have been presented with one microscope. Before that came, in the whole of Mandalay we had not one. With only a few microscopes and medical and laboratory apparatus, we can open some facilities that are closed. It is true that we shall have thirty or forty students crowding around one microscope, but that is better than having none at all. Burma has lost all its bridges. Our roads are just a series of pits. Epidemics are ravaging the countryside. In this situation, we must have hundreds of doctors and engineers qualifying each year. Help from abroad will put courage into us to organize ourselves to meet our needs."

What teen-agers were doing was outstanding. In Yugoslavia, members of the Youth Organization were helping rebuild roads, construct canals, and regulate rivers. Working under the direction of skilled engineers and surveyors, they were learning by doing. When it was decided to build a railway line linking the coal-mining area of Tuzla and the Banovic mines in eastern Bosnia, sixty-two thousand Yugoslav young people had volunteered for two months each. Living in huts they built themselves, doing their own cooking and laundering, in six months they had completed the railroad, including the building of twenty-two bridges and the erecting of twenty-one hundred telegraph and telephone poles.

In Hungary, the young members of the Popular Association of Hungarian Youth were working for their schools. Going out in brigades in the late afternoon and over week ends, they were building school buildings under the direction of experienced carpenters. In Budapest alone there were twenty-four of these brigades; in rural Hungary, over four hundred. Teen-age girl members of the Association, making school equipment, had already produced ten thousand school satchels and four thousand inkpots.

UNESCO decided to do two things with the missions' reports. It would publish them so that the people of many countries might know what they could do to help. And it would establish in UNESCO House a headquarters where voluntary organizations and individual citizens, as well as governments, could obtain further information.

The First Book of Needs and *The Second Book of Needs,* which UNESCO then published, contained a special chapter for each country visited by the missions, telling just how matters stood with their schools, their libraries, and the rest. A list was also given of the specific needs of each. Both books, distributed by UNESCO's National Commissions and by the governments of the member nations, helped answer the people's question: "Just what can we do to help?"

The plan to have an international headquarters of information at UNESCO House proved an excellent one. Twenty-nine world federations at once affiliated themselves with it, including the International Red Cross, the International Boy Scout and Girl Scout organizations, and the Youth Hostels movement. Within three years, seven hundred voluntary organizations in sixty countries were to be working through UNESCO for educational recon-

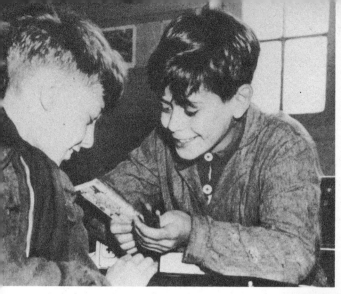

"LOOK WHAT I GOT!"
AT "L'ECOLE DES GARCONS"
EXCLAIMED THIS FRENCH BOY
IN PARIS, THE DAY THE
SCHOOL'S JUNIOR RED CROSS
GIFT BOX ARRIVED
FROM THE UNITED STATES

IT WAS AN HONOR
AT THE SANTOL-GALAS SCHOOL
IN QUEZON CITY,
THE PHILIPPINES, TO BE
ONE OF THE STUDENTS CHOSEN
TO OPEN UP THIS CHEST,
GIFT OF AMERICAN JUNIOR
RED CROSS MEMBERS

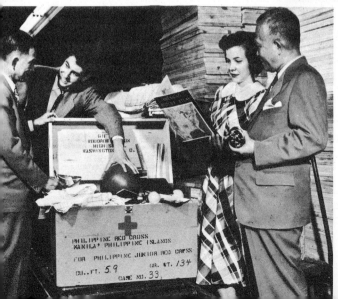

WOODROW WILSON
HIGH SCHOOL STUDENTS
IN WASHINGTON, D.C.,
SHOW TWO VISITING FILIPINO
SUPERINTENDENTS OF SCHOOLS
THEIR JUNIOR RED CROSS
CHEST, A GIFT TO
YOUTH IN THE PHILIPPINES

struction in the countries that still needed help, and more than one hundred million dollars was to be raised by those organizations.

How was this money spent? To rebuild school, college, and university buildings — those of destroyed medical schools, science laboratories, libraries, museums, and the like. To buy equipment for them. To buy books. Wherever these gifts went, the governments and the people matched them with indomitable effort. At many a college, many a medical school, the students themselves did much of the work of rebuilding and installing the equipment.

Helping schools such as Kyria's especially appealed to the young people in the countries where the reconstruction money was raised. They could do something about those appalling totals in the *Books of Needs* — the one hundred and fifty million pencils needed, the seventy-four million, six hundred and seventy thousand notebooks, the millions upon millions of books, to mention only three items on the long list.

Teen-agers around the world got busy. Even small children joined in. Coin boxes in classrooms bulged. Benefit school and club fairs were held. School bands gave concerts. And how the teen-agers did collect! Newspaper clippings, arriving at UNESCO House, showed pictures of them standing beside veritable mountains of pencils in Australia, Canada, Sweden, South Africa, and many other countries.

In the United States, the national headquarters for the work was CIER, the Commission for International Educational Reconstruction, in Washington, D.C. Ably directed by Harold E. Snyder, who made the trip through Greece with Mr. Kenworthy, CIER interested more than three hundred American voluntary organizations in contributing two hundred and fourteen million dollars for educational reconstruction in the devastated countries.

When UNESCO's National Commission was started in the United States, it entered into partnership with CIER. Many American young people sent gifts to the children of Greece because of the UNESCO booklet which was distributed by both CIER and the National Commission — *Marika, the Fate of 340,000 Greek Children.* They learned what they could do for crippled, deaf, and blind youth through UNESCO's *Children, War's Victims — the Education of the Handicapped.*

They collected thousands of books because they read UNESCO's *Libraries in Need,* sending them for forwarding to the Book Center at the Library of Congress. In all, more than four million books were packed and shipped at the Center. Young people's and children's rooms in public and school libraries became headquarters for making treasure chests and filling them with new books for young readers abroad.

Junior Red Cross members were more than busy with their gift boxes, packing up pencils, erasers, chalk, notebooks, and other classroom supplies; with First Aid kits and soccer footballs; never forgetting the teachers, for whom there were sweaters, bath towels, soap, cold cream, and other personal articles. With the gift boxes went correspondence exchange albums, filled with illustrated letters, with clippings from school papers about their sports, their plays, their dramatics. Picture post cards were pasted in, together with descriptions of what American life was like where the senders lived.

In due time, return albums arrived from abroad with the same kinds of letters and pictures. And what up to then had been mere dots on a map became places where new friends lived. Since friends are to be cherished, this was just the beginning. More letters followed. And the correspondence album plan became a permanent part of Junior Red Cross activities.

Through the CIER-UNESCO Commission partnership, classes were able to adopt classes abroad who were busy with the same kinds of special study being enjoyed by the American teen-agers. Future Homemakers of America sent cooking and sewing equipment to domestic science classes; Future Farmers, hoes, spades, and seeds. Carpentry classes sent hammers, saws, and nails. Some groups chose European schools in places from which, generations before, early settlers had come to their own locality in America. When the New Utrecht High School in Brooklyn heard that the Second Commercial School of Utrecht, Holland, needed recording equipment and records, the Brooklyn young people sent them a phonograph, microphone, loud-speaker, and language-teaching records. And again pen friends across the many miles came to know one another.

And schools adopted schools. When the students of the Louis Pasteur Junior High School in Los Angeles, California, decided to adopt a school abroad, they had a faculty UNESCO chairman, Kathryn C. Holsapple, to make the arrangements, for each of the Los Angeles schools has such a chairman through the United Nations plan worked out by Alexander J. Stoddard, Superintendent of Schools and member of the United States National Commission for UNESCO. Miss Holsapple went to see Hilde Flint, representative in Los Angeles of the Austria Women's Association for the United Nations.

Through Miss Flint, the Louis Pasteur School heard about the Bundesreal-gymnasium XVI in the French Zone of Vienna, whose students are teen-agers as are those at Pasteur. Would the students in the Vienna school be interested in the idea? There was no doubt about that when Helen Jewett Rogers, Pasteur's principal, heard from Dr. Norbert Janitschek, the Bundes-realgymnasium's principal. Things started humming at once. Letters arrived in Vienna from one hundred and fifty Pasteur teen-agers, each of whom had chosen a student in the Vienna school for a special pen friend. The Bund-esrealgymnasium teen-agers answered promptly, enclosing snapshots and picture post cards. The Pasteur students brought these letters to school to read aloud in class, and the Austrian young people did the same thing with their American friends' letters.

Both schools had special bulletin boards for the latest news from their correspondents. In Pasteur, there was a big demand in the school library for books and stories about Austria and Vienna. Pasteur Assembly programs featured Austrian songs and folk dances. Pasteur cooking classes produced Austrian dishes. The school's exhibit cases displayed the gifts that the students in Vienna were soon tucking into their letters. Most of these gifts were very simple little handmade articles but all had artistic touches.

Everyone at Pasteur was delighted when word arrived that a new recreation club, which had been organized among the girls at the Bundesreal-gymnasium, had been named the Louis Pasteur Club. "Every club afternoon is started with a lecture or a movie," wrote one of the members to her Los Angeles pen friend. "In the meantime those who like to play can make use of the other room. In the second part of the afternoon those who like to paint or make handicraft gather and make little gifts for abroad. On one of the next club afternoons, a girl will hold a speech about the United States and show us the pictures she has received from her pen friend. Our club library is just at its beginning, and we look forward with very much pleasure to those books and magazines you kindly offered to us.

"Our club is like the International Relations Clubs, and it is the first of its kind in Austria. Our leaders try to connect the young people of the whole world and we are glad that you offered us an opportunity to new friendship. This friendship which starts with correspondence would get further stimula-tions, if perhaps guests from your country coming to Vienna would pay us a visit."

WHEN THE TEEN-AGERS
IN THE LOUIS PASTEUR
JUNIOR HIGH SCHOOL
OF LOS ANGELES
ADOPTED A SCHOOL
IN VIENNA, THEY HELD
A VIENNA WEEK
TO COLLECT GIFTS
FOR THEIR NEW FRIENDS

FIRST, THERE WERE
CORRESPONDENCE
EXCHANGE ALBUMS
— THEN LETTERS FROM
PEN FRIENDS SPEEDING
ACROSS OCEANS

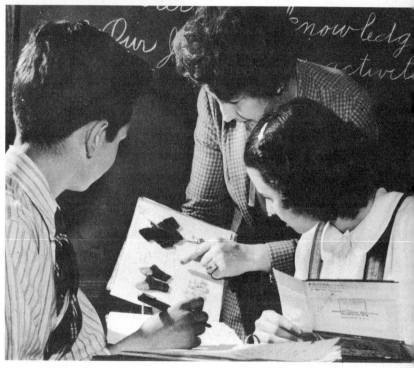

THE LOUIS PASTEUR
STUDENTS FOUND THIS
PICTURE IN THE PACKAGE
WHEN THEIR
VIENNA SCHOOL SENT A
PERSONALLY MADE
CHRISTMAS CAROL
RECORDING

This invitation to visit Vienna was accepted — but that came later. The magazines mentioned in the letter were sent from the Pasteur Parent-Teacher Association, for they, too, joined in the adoption plan, with the Pasteur PTA president finding her own pen friend in the Louis Pasteur Vienna Club's "club mother."

Subscribing to the magazines was the PTA's share in the Pasteur school's Vienna Week. What a week it was! The school's exhibit cases were full of Austrian handicraft, pictures, posters, books — just about everything from Austria that Los Angeles could produce. Every morning Viennese records were played over the school's public-address system. One day was Pencil Collection Day, and more than three thousand pencils were brought in. Coin boxes in the lunch court became so full that they had to be emptied frequently, and in all the school collected two hundred dollars for school supplies of all kinds. There was a headquarters for good used clothing, which filled twenty-eight large boxes when it was packed for shipping. With the clothing, new dress materials were sent.

Inge Beydi, a Freshman at the Bundesrealgymnasium, was chosen to write the school's official letter of thanks. "I should like to thank you all for that wonderful sign of friendship for your Austrian friends," she wrote in English with precise, beautiful penmanship. "When the first pictures of the 'Vienna Week' arrived here, we felt that you did all that collecting for us not as a thing that has to be done, but out of real friendly feelings. You can imagine that this made us more happy, and when the parcels arrived we saw in them a real sign of your friendship for us.

"As president substitute of our club I helped with the opening of the parcels and you can't imagine how enthusiastic we were. We felt that we couldn't open them as quick enough, as it should have been, compared with our curiosity. Those things were so neatly packed and I felt that you did that with love. We enjoyed that looking inside very much and admired every single piece."

Christmas brought the Louis Pasteur students a ten-inch record from their Austrian friends, for which those in the Vienna school had sung and recorded three Christmas carols and two folk songs in German. In the package with the record was a beautifully illuminated manuscript of each song so that the Los Angeles teen-agers might learn to sing them, too. Another large Christmas package from the Vienna school had in it handmade Tyrolean belts, dolls, tea napkins, and bookmarks. Still another contained a beautiful crèche made by "our little ones" from paper and cardboard. At Eastertime, the Bundesrealgymnasium sent a fifty-foot roll of movie film to their Pasteur friends, showing the Vienna boys and girls in several Austrian folk dances. Accompanying the film were full instructions for the teaching of each dance, and drawings to illustrate the various steps. Promptly the Los Angeles Pasteur students began whirling and stomping!

When the KFI radio station in Los Angeles decided to tell about the school adoption idea on its *United Nations Success Story* program, the Louis Pasteur-Bundesrealgymnasium friendship was chosen for dramatization. And when KFI presented a transcription of the broadcast to Pasteur, the students had a copy made for their Vienna school. Did they mail it? No. Miss Holsapple took it to Vienna, where she joined the thirty-three members of the Louis Pasteur Club for a vacation bus tour in the Austrian Alps.

Ali and Fatima had no good times at school, for they had no school, there on the desert in Palestine where they had fled with their parents. They often wished for one, and their mother prayed for it. The things those two got into, with their friends — pushing over tents, tripping people and making them fall on their faces! Keeping Ali and Fatima in did no good except for the time being. Next day they were at it again. Yet who could blame them really, with nothing to do all day long? Perhaps the friends who were bringing the milk and the food would bring a school, too. Their mother certainly hoped so.

Friends did bring a school to Ali and Fatima — not UNICEF, however, but UNESCO. The UNESCO-sponsored schools for Arab refugee young people in Palestine got under way at the time of the 1949 General Conference in Beirut, Lebanon, when a committee of the delegates went out to visit the refugee camps on the desert near by. They returned with a poignant story of how thousands of youth were leading lives as aimless as Ali's and Fatima's. UNESCO then voted to start as many schools in the camps as its budget would allow. Red Cross and American Friends Service Committee field workers, already carrying heavy responsibilities, offered to supervise the schools. And as soon as the plan was announced, governments and organizations added their financial help.

Which explains why to Ali and Fatima, not so very long after UNESCO's

Beirut meetings, the days were no longer dull, meaningless stretches of time. Every morning they rushed out, racing down the long row of tents, past the public scrivener already busy with his writing, past the Mosque standing in its scrupulously clean spot where, several times a day, their white-bearded sheik sang the prayers which the worshipers repeated, past the crude "shops" contrived from rags and old carpets where refugees exchanged and bartered their poor possessions — on, on to the edge of camp and school on the desert sands.

For a while, there was nothing in that school but pupils and their teacher, yet to Ali and Fatima and their friends every lesson was an event. Doing arithmetic sums on the sand with a stick was like a game. Even better were the poetry hours when the whole school chanted together, and the times when their teacher told stories about the Koran, of those who in ancient times traveled far through the desert to the country where wide rivers flowed.

Ali's and Fatima's school at the Mar Elias camp was the first to be opened in Palestine under UNESCO's sponsorship. It was soon followed by others, until there were thirty-one for more than eleven thousand boys and girls in Lebanon, Israel, Syria, and Trans-Jordan. There was no difficulty in finding teachers. Quickly, eagerly, older refugees volunteered. As for pupils — in veritable droves they came running, crowding up. When the girls in the Neuserath Camp school had their BCG vaccinations and their headmistress told them they could go home for the rest of the day, they refused. "We have had enough holidays," they said.

The schools met in all kinds of places — patched-up dwellings, old army barracks, tents, and in the open air. To the teaching of the usual school sub-jects handicraft and agricultural classes were added whenever it was possible. The equipment, when it arrived, was put to immediate use, often as in Gaza, for an unusual kind of geography lesson. The blackboards and chalk, arriving at the Gaza Camp school, had been bought with pennies contributed by South African boys and girls from their pocket money. This money, one hundred pounds in all, had been sent to UNESCO House in Paris from which, in turn, it went to London, where the blackboards and the chalk were bought. The ships bringing the gift cargo to Port Said had sailed one hundred and fifty miles. From Port Said, the blackboards and the chalk had come by truck to Gaza. And the students in the Gaza school traced on their map each step of the long journey.

Letters arriving at UNESCO House from the Palestine schools left no doubt of what the Arab boys and girls thought about them. "It is a joy to see my young people in our classrooms," wrote one teacher, "and gratifying to watch the improvement in their appearance. What they do have to wear is cleaner, their faces are washed, and their hair receives more care. For the boys, this frequently means clipped hair. The girls manage some semblance of tidiness for theirs, and hair ribbons appear, although the lack of combs is something I hope we can remedy soon."

"We are making progress," wrote a supervisor, "even though our pupils are still sitting on stones and sand, for we have a blackboard for every class now and a limited supply of paper. Every boy or girl has a pencil, although pencils and chalk will have to be replaced in all the schools this month. Much of the work is by memorization from the blackboard, for there is still not enough equipment to change that method of teaching. Most classes recite in unison.

"Three football games a week are played. It takes your breath away to see the enthusiasm with which our young people play on these grassless, stony, sunbaked fields. We have forty-five looms operating now with an average of ten pupils learning to weave on each loom. And at the Imam Shafi I Boys' School, we have furnished materials for a class in basket-making and one in broom-making. We use the baskets and brooms in our schools."

When a UNESCO field worker asked Mr. Fattah Nounih what his school of almost two thousand boys and girls in the El Shune camp needed, he had ready the all-too-familiar list he and his thirty-two teachers had drawn up.

"And a school bell, please," he concluded.

"Do you really mean a *bell?*" the worker asked.

"Certainly," replied Mr. Nounih. "A school bell is most essential." (He got it, a gift from an anonymous friend who heard the story.)

Which is why when UNESCO sent out an appeal for its schools in Palestine, the booklet was called *A Schoolbell in the Wilderness*.

PESTALOZZI VILLAGE
AT TROGEN,
SWITZERLAND,
IS THEIR HOME
TO WAR ORPHANS OF
MANY NATIONALITIES —
A UNITED EUROPE
IN MINIATURE

THE SILVI MARINA, ITALY,
BOYS THEMSELVES
DID A GREAT DEAL
OF THE WORK
WHEN THEIR NEW
BOYS TOWN WAS BUILT

FIFTY TEEN-AGERS
OF FIVE NATIONALITIES
HAD GREAT FUN
AT THEIR INTERNATIONAL
HOLIDAY CAMP,
MOULIN VIEUX, FRANCE

LIVING AND LEARNING
TOGETHER

It was on Christmas Eve, 1945, that a little priest, Don Guido Visendas, arrived at the small village of Lanciano, Italy, where a gang of lawless boys, left homeless by the war, had been shut up by the authorities, grown desperate with their marauding. After explaining to the officials that he had come to help, Don Guido was given the key to the half-ruined stable of the Santa Chiara barracks.

Opening the stable door, he was greeted with jeers and catcalls from the boys who, ragged and flea-bitten, lay shivering on the bare stone floor. Calmly Don Guido settled down to live with them. At first, even when he brought them food and clothing, they continued to jeer. When he started to clean the stable, they made no move to help. But when he began to plaster the broken walls, a few joined in. And the day he arrived with brightly colored paint, all became excited. Soon gay flowers, painted by the boys themselves, looked down on their stable home, their *villaggio*, of which they now were proud.

From homeless boy to homeless boy throughout the Lanciano countryside word spread of what was happening at the villaggio. Eighty more boys between the ages of five and eighteen arrived, and it became necessary for Don Guido to take over the entire floor of the barracks. With these new-comers, a serious problem arose. Some went out at night to rob nearby homes. To be sure, they were after food for all the villaggio, but it was stealing nevertheless, and the townspeople complained bitterly.

Calling the boys together, Don Guido said, "I must be free to get the food, the clothing, and the other things you need. After this, you are to be responsible for what happens here." The boys drew up a constitution, estab-lished a court, elected a mayor. There were no more robberies.

With more than a hundred boys to look after, it was difficult to make ends meet. Often Don Guido was at his wit's end to find enough food for them and for the teachers of the villaggio school he soon started. Italian friends were helping, and organizations such as Don Suisse. But the vil-laggio needed more, much more. It was Don Suisse's suggestion that Don Guido and the villaggio's fifteen-year-old mayor go to Switzerland to tell about the villaggio and its needs.

When Don Guido announced that he and the mayor would be away for a time, a meeting was held to vote on who was to be acting mayor during their absence. The boy of the villaggio's choice refused the responsibility. "I would make too many mistakes," he declared. Whereupon his friends de-creed by unanimous vote: "We hereby give you the right to make mistakes." He accepted, and Don Guido and the mayor left for Switzerland.

By the time they returned, the Swiss schools had adopted the villaggio, and Swiss youth were enthusiastically collecting funds, food, and clothing to help keep Don Guido's boys together. With this aid and that from the Italian Government and voluntary organizations, Don Guido and his boys managed to go on. When Father Flanagan of Boys Town, Nebraska, sent a check for a thousand dollars, Don Guido put it into shop equipment and added carpentry, tailoring, and shoemaking to the reading, writing, arith-metic, and the other subjects already being taught in the villaggio school. In their tailor shop, the boys made clothes from remnants of discarded United States Army tents.

In March 1948 the villaggio received bad news. The barracks were needed for other purposes and they must move. Learning of their predica-ment, the Italian Government offered them a piece of land on the nearby hills of Silvi Marina, overlooking the Adriatic Sea. After a committee of the boys had reported favorably on the location, it was decided to build a new home there and to call it Boys Town.

Many friends shared in building the new Boys Town. Don Suisse supplied prefabricated parts for the five simple buildings. A French architect volunteered his services. UNICEF, in partnership with the Italian Government, provided supplementary meals. And the boys themselves worked like Trojans, sleeping on the open beach, each with only one blanket and no pillow, but happy that step by step their Boys Town was becoming a reality. Before the buildings were finished they had a big vegetable garden growing. And when, at last, they moved in, it didn't matter that they had no lights, that water must be carried a long distance. They were together in their own town.

Throughout Europe, and in Burma, India, and Malaya, warmhearted men and women were gathering together groups of boys and girls left homeless by the war. Although differing in various ways, these youth communities were alike in trying to give their young citizens as much of a real home as they could, physical and medical care, an education, and responsibility in running the affairs of the community.

The idea of such youth communities was not new. More than fifty years before, William R. George, an American, had started one of the first of them, the George Junior Republic, in Freeville, New York. Others followed, and many grown men and women today are grateful for all that was given them in their growing-up years at such places as the *Cité Joyeuse,* the garden city for orphans at Molenbeek, Brussels; in the Werkplaats Children's Community at Bilthoven, Netherlands; in the Bernardo Homes of the United Kingdom; and at Father Flanagan's Boys Town.

Now new leaders were struggling to carry out the same plan, and it *was* a struggle. There was Pastor Sztehlo, who was employing every effort to make a home in Budapest for boys and girls whose parents could not be traced. There was Scoutmaster Paul LeLièvre, at Ker-Goat in Brittany, often well-nigh desperate as he tried to keep his boys' farm community on its feet. There were Mr. and Mrs. Henri Julien, two teachers who in their *République d'Enfants* at Moulin Vieux near Grenoble were looking after young Spanish exiles, as well as German, Czech, French, and Polish young people and children. There were Mr. and Mrs. Pit Kruger, German refugees themselves, who, with the help of the people of Mosset in the Pyrenees, had started an international hostel in a stable. And many more.

Like the teachers UNESCO was helping, they needed to get together, to share experiences and problems. They needed to let the peoples of the world know about what they were doing, and to receive help. Early in 1948 UNESCO sent out invitations to a conference of youth community leaders to be held that summer at Pestalozzi Village in Trogen, Switzerland.

Pestalozzi Village, another of the new youth communities, is a United Europe in miniature. Its young citizens live in chalets, each chalet for those of one nationality and with a house parent from their own country— a French chalet for French boys and girls, a German chalet for the Germans, and so on. First suggested by Walter Corti, a Zurich editor, the idea for such an international village was taken up by the Swiss Youth Organization, *Pro Juventute.* It was a plan that quickly fired the imagination of the generous Swiss. By 1946 enough money had been contributed so that a site could be chosen. Beautiful Trogen was selected and it was decided to call the youth community the *Kinderdorf Pestalozzi,* after a famous Swiss pioneer educator.

When the people of Trogen heard the news, they donated ten acres of their common land and the farmhouse on it to the new village. Neighbor farmers built a road and put in a water and drainage system. Hundreds of volunteers, many of them in their teens, appeared to dig the foundations for the chalets and to help build them. Sixty teen-agers from nearby Heiden chopped down a huge tree and hauled it seven miles to the Trogen sawmill to be cut into boards. And boys and girls all over Switzerland followed suit.

In the summer of 1946 one hundred and twelve war orphans from France, Poland, Austria, Hungary, and Germany were able to move in, each group in its own chalet. With the money now coming from overseas friends, such gifts as oranges from Palestine, honey from Australia, twenty tons of coal from Poland also arrived. Trogen mothers sewed and knitted for the young citizens, and their children collected seeds which the Pestalozzi boys and girls planted in their vegetable gardens.

In each chalet the native language of its young residents was spoken, but this did not keep Pestalozzi's citizens from understanding one another. The house parents often laughed over the curious sign languages they evolved, and marveled at how rapidly enough words were picked up for animated conversations. Singing bees were more than popular when they all learned the songs of other countries, and the dancing hours when everybody whirled and stomped in everybody else's folk dances.

Those in their teens, given a great deal of responsibility for running the Village, promptly made a rule that no matter where a boy or girl came from, he or she was not to be made to "feel different." Even the smallest children got the idea. One day, when a twelve-year-old German boy arrived, after having walked all the way from Bremen, it was the Polish children, who had suffered most from the Germans, who made him a pair of skis so that he could join them in their sport.

Experienced teachers came to the Village to work in the school which all attended. The youngest children were taught in their own language. For those over twelve, German was the language used. And as in Don Guido's Boys Town, there were workshops and craft classes as well as those in mathematics, history, science, and literature.

UNESCO's conference invitation to come to Trogen was accepted by fourteen leaders of youth communities in six different countries. Joining with them were eleven experienced educators from six countries, including the United States, whose representative was Dr. Carleton Washburne, international president of the New Education Fellowship. In all, eleven of UNESCO's member nations were represented.

From the first meeting the thoughts of the delegates were not only with boys and girls made homeless by the war but with those in all countries to whom the youth community plan could bring so much. And they talked of the youth of tomorrow as well as of today. *Homeless Children,* published by UNESCO shortly after the conference, gives their discussions on the ways and means by which youth communities may be effectively planned and carried on. Sent out to the struggling new leaders, it brought them valued suggestions and encouragement. Through it, too, new youth communities were started.

Children's Communities: A Way of Life for War's Victims, which UNESCO also published, told the peoples of the world about Pestalozzi Village, Don Guido's Boys Town, and others, giving a list of sixty-three youth communities in all, together with their addresses and their urgent needs. Again the generous peoples responded, and financial help arrived.

Most important of all was UNESCO's announcement that an International Federation of Children's Communities had been organized at the conference. Through this Federation today help is being extended to youth community leaders in all parts of the world, from the Federation's world headquarters in Trogen, which UNESCO helped establish. Each year many letters arrive from those interested in starting youth communities, and each is answered with practical suggestions. Six months' training courses are given at Trogen by experts in all phases of youth and child care, and among those who attend are men and women whose presence has been made possible by UNESCO fellowships.

When Henri Julien was getting ready to leave the *République d'Enfants* at Moulin Vieux to attend the UNESCO Conference in Trogen, he was visited by a delegation of the République's citizens with a proposal. "Why can't we boys and girls have an international meeting, too?" they asked him. "We could have a camp and hold it here. Please, Papa Torchok. It would be such fun." Papa Torchok is their name for M. Julien.

When Papa Torchok told those at UNESCO about the suggestion, it was met with enthusiasm, and plans were soon under way for a UNESCO-sponsored Holiday Camp to be held at Moulin Vieux that summer. The boys and girls at Moulin Vieux spent many hours on the invitations, which obviously must be extra-special. Printing them on their own presses, they painted pictures on each, illustrating the fun they would all have together. Fifty teen-agers from youth communities in Belgium, France, Hungary, Italy, and Switzerland accepted, with UNESCO helping make the trip possible for them.

It was, as the boys and girls of Moulin Vieux had predicted, great fun. Sports, dramatics, stunt parties, song fests were the order of the day, and talking things over around the campfire every evening. That they spoke different languages was no more of a handicap than at Pestalozzi. They managed.

One night, at campfire, one of the campers suggested: "Let's have an international organization. You know, writing to each other, exchanging our newspapers and all that, and getting together like this as often as we can."

Everyone was enthusiastic. Those from Pestalozzi Village told about the visit they had had from John Finnerty, teen-age mayor of the Children's Village at Dobbs Ferry, New York, in the United States. Their own friendship

INTERNATIONAL WORK CAMPERS
CONSTRUCT A NEW PLAYGROUND
FOR THE NEIGHBORHOOD CENTER
OF LUDWIGSHAFEN, GERMANY

COLLEGE STUDENT CAMPERS OF FOUR
NATIONALITIES HELP THE PEOPLE OF
GRINS, AUSTRIA, REBUILD THEIR VILLAGE

TEPPA SITTANENE OF
FINLAND WAS A SPECIAL
ASSET TO HER WORK
CAMP, FOR SHE WAS AN
EXPERT AT BRUSH-PILING

TWO UNITED STATES CAMPERS AND
THE JAMAICA BOYS TOWN CITIZENS
START ON THE ROOF OF THE TOWN'S
NEW DINING SHED AND KITCHEN

with those in the Dobbs Ferry Village had started when the boys there sent their Christmas-tree decorations to Pestalozzi, a gift which meant a big sacrifice on the part of the Americans. Ever since, letters had been speeding back and forth. And when, with help from UNESCO in planning his trip, Mayor Finnerty left the United States to visit youth communities in Italy, France, Germany, and other European countries, the *Pestalozzi Kinderdorf* was high on his itinerary.

Having Mayor Finnerty with them had been wonderful, the Pestalozzi campers said. Yes, all decided, they would work for their own international organization. And when they told their UNESCO friends about the idea, UNESCO promised to help.

At the very time when the Moulin Vieux campers were talking over their day, others in Europe were discussing theirs — campers in Austria, Belgium, Denmark, England, Finland, Germany, Holland, Italy, Norway, the Saar, Sweden, and Switzerland, as well as in France. What they had to tell was very different. They had had singing, yes, and comradeship, but they did not mention a morning's swimming meet, afternoon dramatics or crafts, because for them every hour had been full of something far different.

Going back to their tents, their huts, or their dormitories, they wrote home about what they had been doing. "The work is coming along well, I think. The reservoir is really looking like a reservoir, and one group of us has begun digging a foundation to level the road some more so a bridge can be built." "Our team of fourteen members is helping build a stone house from the gaunt walls on, to make a youth center."

"We are two Americans here in our camp near Berlin, where we are working with the boys of a school on a building they need. All in all, seven nations are represented but we have more 'Berliners,' as we call them, than the others." "Way up north in Lapland is the location of our summer camp. It is so thrilling — youth from Finland, France, Britain, Norway, Denmark, and America, camping and working together."

How had these camps happened? It all goes back to a Swiss engineer, Pierre Ceresole, of the Friends' faith, who in 1919 conceived the idea of having young people of many nations camp together during the summer, spending their days in reconstruction work. He felt sure that if youth, even those from countries with long histories of hatred, could work side by side in voluntary, unselfish, constructive service, it would be a step toward peace. "The glad and free co-operation of those who are working and living for others is the true miracle," he said, "capable of making all others possible."

He named the movement *Service Civil International*, and many young people quickly joined. In the first International Work Camp, which he organized in 1920, Pierre Ceresole inspired both French and German youth to join in clearing the rubble, and building peasant huts near Verdun. When, in 1928, the Rhine flooded in Lichtenstein, more than seven hundred young people from twenty-two countries answered the emergency call, even though the summons read: "The week's work will be forty-eight hours. It will be hard. Volunteers will be lodged in tents, barns, and empty buildings. Work will have to be done in the rain."

Within a few years organizations from many countries were sending out groups to join in what was now known as the International Voluntary Work Camps movement. Summer after summer their number grew, with many kinds of organizations sponsoring them. Although interrupted in some countries by World War II, the camps continued in others. By the summer of 1949 there were upward of nine hundred and fifty of these International Work Camps, from Lapland to Crete, from Jamaica to Japan. Work camps in Central, North, and South America, in Africa, in Asia, Europe, and the Middle East, among them a number that UNESCO itself had organized.

Each of the projects on which they worked had been chosen in consultation with the various governments or national organizations. Because the work itself was "rugged," as one camper put it, the majority were young people in their twenties. More than fifty thousand youth, in a single summer, building and repairing roads; working on flood-control and reforestation projects; doing medical, social, and educational work; building and repairing schools, hospitals, churches, playgrounds, youth centers, and youth hostels.

In Holland today an important dyke holds firm because campers from England, France, and Finland repaired it. In Austria teachers can go for special training to a center that twenty-five campers from eight countries made for them from an old castle. In Yugoslavia everyone who takes the train from Samac to Sarajevo goes over a railroad bed constructed by five thousand work campers who joined the Yugoslav Youth Organization in one of the largest of the work camps. Each day after work many gave an hour to teaching twenty thousand fellow campers to read and write. In the United States the Navaho Indians in Utah have school dormitories built by their fellow Americans and those from other countries. During a single summer, work campers came to the United States from Austria, Canada, China, Denmark, England, Finland, Italy, Luxembourg, Mexico, Germany, Norway, and Sweden to join in work camp projects here.

Being in a work camp brings rewarding if strenuous days. "Seventeen of us helped resettle *évacuées* in the Tervola district of Finland," wrote Leta Cromwell of the American Friends Service Committee in an article for *The Junior League Magazine,* entitled "Pick and Shovel Diplomats." "Our job for the summer was to assist five especially needy families. The toy train bearing us — some Swiss, Danes, Swedes, Americans, and eleven Finns — had ambled up from Helsinki through two days of meadows, pines, sapphire lakes, and cloudless sky. It was a seven-kilometer walk to the camp site, with baggage, on a sandy road through swamps.

"Nights don't vary much when camping, I expect. They're a losing battle with insects, the cold, and the vise-like embrace of your sleeping bag. You rise at 6 A.M., and wash in the river. Breakfast isn't inspiring — weak tea, oatmeal, hardtack. For lunch there's vegetable soup and potatoes; for dinner, oatmeal made elegant with lingenberries, soup, and hardtack. Actually, we were eating as did the people of the country — and even the Americans survived!

"Typical of the families we tried to help was a man, his wife, and five children under twelve. He had been evacuated twice. The newly constructed bathhouse, in which the whole family lived, a snarly dog, and a thin pig constituted his possessions. But like so many people one meets abroad, he was looking forward, not back. 'One day when the new settlement is finished, I shall be postmaster,' he told us gaily as he passed us the coffee seasoned with salt which the Finns pressed on us every morning and afternoon. A tiny man in huge hip boots, he was starting on the foundations of his house, in that wilderness of peat bogs, dwarf birches, and scraggly woods.

"The friendliness of the villagers is one of the rewards for the hours of work and inconvenience. It's the volunteer aspect that startles and touches them. At every work camp I visited after I left Tervola I found the same thing. The people marveled that a locomotive engineer would spend his two-week vacation leveling a playground, a young teacher clearing rubble to put a hospital back into running order, that university students would give up a carefree vacation to rebuild a school. And to think that the campers take no pay, that voluntary organizations join in providing for their expenses!

"'All that way!' a local carpenter exclaims. 'Someday I'll come to America and help you.'

"A blacksmith refuses pay after he has repaired a work camp spade. 'You work without wages,' he says. 'I can't accept anything for helping you.'

"An honor I shall never forget was being made godmother to a Finnish baby boy. I took the best gift I could find to the christening, a cake of soap tied with a red ribbon. It could have been pure gold, so ecstatic was its reception. Yes, we had many social events. With a coffee party or a 'sing,' or with volley ball, we entertained the village and they entertained us.

"The closest ties, of course, develop in each camp itself among the members. At first there is shyness, sometimes even suspicion and hostility. But after eight weeks of working together: 'We'll be sorry to see you go,' exclaimed one group of villagers. 'You seem so happy!'

"I had many occasions to be proud of my compatriots as I traveled from work camp to work camp. In theory, work campers are expected to know something of the language of the country in which they plan to serve, but hardly Finnish with its sixteen cases! Yet I met one American girl sitting on a log two hundred miles north of the Arctic Circle, sipping coffee with a small Lapp couple, her blond curls glistening in the silver northern sunlight, who in a ceaseless flow of Finnish was swapping jokes with the old man about reindeer."

When the work campers left Finland, a farmer wrote them, "Now I am writing some words to you good campers. At first I want to thank you for helping us in many kinds of important work. You have voluntarily come here to help us from different countries and have understood our needs — how we have had to build everything anew, fields as well as houses. I want also to thank all who have arranged these camps.

"We shall have many good memories of you. When we visit the places where you have been working, we will think of you. You have been like the migratory bird. You came in the spring, stayed here for the summer working with us, and now that autumn has come you leave us. You go back to your own countries and to your own work and we feel very sad at your leaving. May God bless you all, both on your journey and at your home."

It was in the summer of 1947 that UNESCO field workers first went out to visit International Work Camps. Going to Belgium, Czechoslovakia, France, and Poland, everywhere they found youth from many countries coming close in understanding friendship as they camped and worked together. Joining in the after-work and week-end hours of sitting under the trees and talking things over, they saw how valuable these discussions were. And they found much good work being done, some of it inevitably better than elsewhere, but on the whole all of it more than creditable.

But they learned, too, of the many difficulties. Difficulties in finding the right kinds of project, in making travel arrangements, in procuring tools and equipment. And ever and always the difficulties of the voluntary organizations in raising enough money to keep the projects going.

"Can't we get together to talk over our problems?" work camp leaders everywhere asked.

UNESCO arranged for them to do so, sending out an invitation to meet at UNESCO House in Paris. This meeting, held in 1948, was attended by delegates from nine countries, representing nineteen organizations sponsoring the camps. Representatives of the International Labour Organization of the UN also attended, for it is important that all work camp projects be planned in accordance with its standards. It was then that a permanent Work Camp Co-ordinating Committee was formed, with year-round headquarters at UNESCO House, where monthly executive meetings are held. Here letters continuously arrive from organizations in all parts of the world who wish to sponsor work camps, and every letter is answered with practical suggestions. Letters come from young people, too, asking how they may become work campers, and each is told where to write for information in his own country. To help those interested in starting new work camps, UNESCO has published a handbook, *Organizing International Voluntary Work Camps*.

As its share in the camp discussions, UNESCO places in as many of the camps as possible UNESCO libraries in each of which are upward of two hundred and fifty books and pamphlets on world affairs, including publications of the United Nations. In the winter the books are placed in youth centers and schools.

After the camping season of 1949 UNESCO sent out an invitation to a meeting of the campers themselves, to be held at L'Abbaye de Royaumont in France. Putting away their picks and shovels, storing wheelbarrows for the winter, forty-eight delegates representing fourteen nationalities met for three days.

It was a splendid conference. "The one thing that has been brought out most clearly for me here at Royaumont is that our movement is not a closed one," one of the delegates said. "We are many organizations, differing on many points, but when we can get together, there is a great deal we can teach and learn from each other."

At their last session the delegates sent a message to UNESCO's General Conference, which concluded with these words: "We, as you, represent people of many nations. We, as you, hope that the accomplishments of this week will provide not only practical means but real inspiration to men and women everywhere who by their example and activities are attempting to make international friendship and understanding a lasting reality."

Work campers speaking with work campers, united in their common aim: "Building peace through small international groups of volunteers working, living, and learning together."

IT'S A LIVELY GAME
FOR THE FINNISH BOYS AND GIRLS AT PESTALOZZI VILLAGE

AS A REWARD FOR THEIR MODEL
SECURITY COUNCIL MEETING, SPLENDIDLY PRESENTED IN CANADA, THESE
STUDENTS OF LOYALTY SCHOOL, HUXLEY, WERE GIVEN A TRIP TO LAKE SUCCESS

THROUGHOUT THE UNITED STATES, YOUNG PEOPLE
DISCUSS THE UNITED NATIONS CHARTER AND THE DECLARATION OF HUMAN RIGHTS

BENI ABBES, ALGERIA, WAS FIRST
STOP FOR UNESCO'S EXPEDITION

THE PEOPLES SPEAK
WITH THE PEOPLES

"We rely on UNESCO, but we know that UNESCO gives preference to those who prove that they can help themselves. So we have decided to show what we can do, and we have agreed on a program of international exchange of youngsters. Next summer boys and girls from Finnish, Danish, Dutch, French, and Swiss Science Clubs will visit each other and make personal contacts with the friends across the borders with whom, thanks to UNESCO, they have already begun to correspond."

Twenty-two-year-old Kees Meijers of the Netherlands was speaking, saying good-by to his hosts at UNESCO House where he had been meeting with other young Science Club leaders from nine countries. It had been an exciting three days, learning what young scientists were doing from Korea to Copenhagen, from Prague to Paraguay. They had heard about the young cave explorers, the speleogists of France; the young astronomers of Brazil; the young agriculturalists — the 4-H's and the Future Farmers' Clubs — of the United States; and many other groups. They had spent all the time they possibly could at the exhibition arranged for them, Science Clubs at Work. They had discussed how their clubs back home could use the "prize questions" idea of the Finnish Clubs, how they could organize science fairs, such as those held by the Danish youth, how they could conduct an annual talent search like that of the sixteen thousand Science Clubs of America. And they had been delighted to learn that in five years the member Science Clubs among high school young people in India had jumped from one to more than four hundred.

For all the delegates, the high point of their meetings was that at which UNESCO's Director-General, Jaime Torres Bodet, spoke. Succeeding Julian Huxley as head of UNESCO, dynamic Mr. Torres Bodet brought to his new position valuable and long experience as Minister of Education and Minister of Foreign Affairs in Mexico where his fine work for the education of his country's children, young people, and adults commanded world-wide attention and admiration.

Speaking to the Science Club leaders, Mr. Torres Bodet said: "Though a discovery is not the more meritorious for being made by a young inventor, we cannot help a special feeling of admiration at the thought that before the age of thirty, Joseph Black was carrying out his famous investigations into carbon dioxide, Einstein was formulating his theory of relativity. Last year, the laureate of the American Science Talent Search was only fifteen, and he had already discovered a very important method of synthesizing certain organic compounds.

"All these examples may fire the imagination of young people and draw them into your clubs. Yours is the rare privilege of disseminating, humanizing, and advancing the cause of science. It enables you to help train men and women who will not be mere scientists but citizens with deeper insight into the possibilities and dangers of the world today. Whether they make a name for themselves through far-famed discoveries or merely perform a humble yet necessary task, the members of your clubs will have this in common: they will together have fought against ignorance and prejudice, worked methodically with ever-open minds, faithfully carried out their task, whether great or small, and with their deeper knowledge of the world about them, will better understand the bonds which unite mankind in a common destiny."

News of the young science leaders' meetings appeared in UNESCO's weekly radio script. It was published in newspapers and bulletins, and in three languages in the three different editions of its lively and fascinating monthly paper, *The UNESCO Courier*, from which this account was taken. For UNESCO, as part of its work in the field of science, encourages starting new Science Clubs among young people, as well as helping those already organized in the various countries. It has made a survey of where these clubs are at work and what they are doing, and thus has information at hand with which to answer the letters that come in asking how to organize Science Clubs. In France and Belgium the National Commissions of UNESCO have special committees at work organizing more of these clubs among their youth. When UNESCO prepared a series of scientific exhibits to be sent out by car in Latin-American countries, one of the exhibits featured the activities of youth's Science Clubs in various parts of the world.

Young Science Club members eagerly follow what UNESCO is doing as it works with scientists around the world and with their international and national organizations. They read about its conferences of experts on the Protection of Nature, on High Altitude and Arid Zone research, on the popularization of science. And many a young person, hearing that a UNESCO fellowship has been awarded to a scientist in his own country, resolves that after he has completed his education and gained experience in the scientific field of his choice, he, too, will apply for this valuable study abroad.

Scientists know that they may look to UNESCO for information of all kinds. Teachers and research workers find at UNESCO House up-to-date word about the best available laboratory equipment and so have the advantage of buying wisely when they install a new laboratory or re-equip an old one.

The specialists of UNESCO are working so that word of important discoveries and developments may quickly go out to scientists everywhere, so that word about them will no longer be delayed and human lives thus lost that might otherwise have been saved through the new knowledge. It was only by accident some time ago that a nutritionist in Asia came upon an announcement in a publication from Jamaica describing the successful use of yeast in combating famine.

To take the "accident" out of this situation is UNESCO's aim. In order to do so, it is encouraging more complete publication of what are known as scientific abstracts. For years, upward of a thousand scientific organizations have been issuing these abstracts which are short translated summaries of the many articles published. The summaries are then sent out to the subscribers of the abstracting bulletins. Outstanding in this work has been that in the field of chemistry, which has regularly summarized some five thousand articles written in thirty-one different languages. But there had been no comprehensive plan for all the great field of science.

Now there is such a plan. At a conference called by UNESCO to consider the abstracting situation and attended by one hundred and forty-seven scientists and librarians from twenty-eight countries — a group speaking fifteen different languages — steps were taken to fill the gaps. In their discussions the delegates discovered such things as the fact that dozens of scientific journals were being published in the Middle East about which the scientists of the West had never even heard. In some important fields, almost no abstracting at all has been done — in meteorology, fisheries, and special branches of botany and zoology.

As with so many of the United Nations' long-term plans, this one of UNESCO's for thorough scientific abstracting will take years to complete. But a start has been made. The publishers of scientific periodicals around the world have begun to come together.

Information about new scientific developments goes out from UNESCO House to its Field Science Offices which have been established in different parts of the world so that those living in the various regions may get such information more quickly. Scientists young and old, governments, organizations, and educators look to these offices for all kinds of help. Among the first to be set up were those in Montevideo for Latin America; in Manila for East Asia; in Delhi for South Asia; in Cairo for the Middle East. Others are to follow. Answering questions that come in by mail, making arrangements for the scientists in their regions to get together, seeing that the missions of visiting scientific specialists are looked after, keep the Field Science Service staff busy from morning till night.

The office files are full of all kinds of information, including scientific abstracts. But if they do not have at hand what will answer some question that comes in, they have the world to call upon. They never can tell what they will be asked. From Uruguay may arrive a request for information about the teaching of science in high schools; from Argentine, one for word about photocopies and microfilms on mathematics; from Colombia, about geography congresses. Great Britain may ask for a list of the Societies for the

Advancement of Science; Egypt for help in the purchase of a veterinary X-ray unit; Iraq on how to obtain a deep-sea thermometer; Lebanon for a list of works on cosmic rays. Indo-China may offer marine specimens to any marine biological station which, in exchange for the specimens, will send books on scientific apparatus.

UNESCO's booklet, *Science Liaison*, gives a vivid picture of these Field Science Offices in action, with descriptions of a typical day in each. Each office works closely with FAO, a partnership that often brings about an interesting bit of teamwork. When a certain fast-growing water hyacinth was choking Indonesia's inland waterways, the government wrote in distress, asking what could be done about this weed that was obstructing navigation and killing the fish. After word was sent them about the best weed killer to use, a new difficulty cropped up: the disposal of the enormous bulk of dead and decaying hyacinth weeds. At this juncture, the office heard from FAO field workers that western Bengal needed fertilizer for its work in reviving its barren soil. Not long after, Bengalese farmers had an ample supply of fine fertilizer — dead hyacinth plants! And Indonesia still had plenty for its own use.

Any morning when you go to your science class in school, you may know that somewhere in the world UNESCO is at work on whatever science subject you are studying, whether astronomy, biology, chemistry, earth science, or physics. As you do your laboratory experiments, researchers in other laboratories are carrying on projects that money from UNESCO's budget has helped make possible. In a single year UNESCO helped with one hundred and forty-three of these projects, as they were initiated by fourteen different International Unions of scientists, including the International Union of Scientific Radio.

One of UNESCO's scientists wrote so vividly about what he was seeing and learning in one of its special projects that the students in fifteen thousand British schools felt they were with him out on the desert. He was Ritchie Calder, science editor of the London *News Chronicle* and member of the United Kingdom National Commission for UNESCO. The journey he took was planned at UNESCO House as part of its Arid Regions research activities. He traveled over fifteen thousand miles through deserts from Beni-Abbès in Algeria, along the North African coast line to Egypt, Bagdad, and Teheran, on to Israel and Cyprus.

Before he left, thousands of British youth, from children in the primary grades up to the students in Balliol College, Oxford University, themselves got ready for the trip. They learned why UNESCO had planned it. "People cannot live on the food raised on only two thirds of the earth," Mr. Calder told them. "We need to use it all, In short, we need the deserts. I am going to see what is being done to reclaim them."

Each classroom had a copy of Mr. Calder's itinerary and a list of books recommended by him as interesting reading about the countries he was to visit. Each had a wall map in color, presented by the National Commission and the *News Chronicle,* together with small picture stickers to paste on the map as Mr. Calder went along.

Mr. Calder left London with a photographer. Starting from a desert laboratory in the Algerian Sahara, each day he wrote an article about his latest adventures. Published in forty-three newspapers in thirty-two countries, his accounts gave to thousands of young people and adults the fascinating story of what the desert scientists of today are doing as they combat soil erosion, develop effective fertilizers and irrigation methods, and carry on experiments. And at each place he stopped, the corresponding sticker symbol went onto the wall maps in British classrooms. Mr. Calder called his series of articles *Men against the Desert,* later using the same title for his book in which they are collected. And as he traveled on, he knew that the victory against the sand and the winds can be won, if the peoples will it.

One moonlight night on a desert plateau above the Kasserine Gap, he talked with Charles Saumagne, Tunisian Inspector-General, whom he calls a "Veteran Man against the Desert."

"Tell me that there are ten men in the world who believe that the desert can be made to bear fruit and will redeem the stupidities of mankind, and I will die happy," the General said.

By the time Mr. Calder completed his journey, he was able to write: "Now I can give Charles Saumagne not ten but hundreds — men and women whom I know by name, slaving sacrificially in the desert. They not only believe but are doing, acting not only in faith and knowledge but from results. . . . All through the deserts of North Africa and the Middle East I have seen men triumphant against the desert. I have seen desert places blossoming because man has checked wandering men, wandering sand, and wandering winds. I have learned countless lessons and found abundant hope."

ENGLISH SCHOOLBOYS HAD MANY QUESTIONS FOR RITCHIE CALDER WHEN HE CAME
BACK TO LONDON FROM HIS JOURNEY THROUGH THE DESERT

TO CARRY ON
THEIR EXPERIMENT,
THESE YOUNG
SCIENTISTS
OF SZEGED, HUNGARY,
IMPROVISED A BURNER
FROM AN
ELECTRIC-LIGHT BULB

Among the many who followed Mr. Calder's articles with special interest were the young people and adults in Great Britain and other countries who belong to groups discussing *Food and People*. This is a series of booklets published by UNESCO on the subject FAO has shown to be so crucial. "Enough food for everybody will not become an actuality until the peoples of the world decide that it *must* be accomplished," says the introduction to the series, "and make up their minds *how* in general it must be done."

Through UNESCO, many discussion groups in an increasing number of countries are being organized around these booklets that include one written by Margaret Mead of the American Museum of Natural History, *Food and the Family*.

In Holland, the Youth Hostels movement has adopted the theme for week-end discussions. In Great Britain, the National Union of Students put *Food and People* on a UNESCO Day program in London. UNESCO has prepared special material for work camps in Europe and sent pamphlets to the Farm Service Force of the Y.M.C.A. in Canada, where young people not only have contributed their own labor to increasing food production, but have also sought to learn how their efforts fit into the world picture. In the United States, high school students are joining in the discussions, 4-H and Future Farmers members, young people's International Relations Clubs, United Nations Youth Chapters, and others. American adults, too, are holding meetings in their organizations on this urgent world problem.

When G. G. Fellowes, principal of the Loyalty School in Huxley, Alberta, Canada, came back to his students from welfare work in Europe, he had a new plan for them. He had heard that young people were presenting model General Assembly and Security Council meetings, and he proposed to his teen-agers that they do the same thing. When they enthusiastically voted to do so, they wrote to the UN Department of Public Information for suggestions. With the envelopeful that shortly arrived, they set to work.

They and Mr. Fellowes had not the slightest idea then that word of what they were doing would spread across Canada, that they would go on the radio with it, that they would be given a trip to Lake Success to see the United Nations in action, that they would visit the White House and President Truman. Yet that is what happened.

The Loyalty School young people worked hard on their model Security

Council meeting and were pleased when their audience of parents and others living in and around Huxley were most complimentary. They were pleased, too, when they received invitations to come to nearby communities to repeat their meeting and delighted that the schools there invariably took up the plan for themselves. When newspapers printed accounts of what they were doing, Mr. Fellowes began to get letters even from distant points in Canada. More came in after the Loyalty Security Council group appeared at a banquet in Red Deer, Altoona, and station CKRD broadcast the program. It was also recorded and sent out by other stations, with the result that the Alberta Teachers' Association in Edmonton published a series of articles about the Loyalty School UN work. The trip to Lake Success and the White House was a gift in appreciation of what one small country school has done in helping its country's citizens become acquainted with the UN.

The Loyalty School story is part of a much longer one that tells of UNESCO's partnership with the youth of the world in their schools. That story is being written at UNESCO House as the educator specialists send out letters in answer to the many questions from member countries about how their schools may be made more effective for their young people and children. It is being written around the world as the missions go out to study the schools of various countries and make plans for their betterment — missions to Afghanistan, the Philippines, Thailand, and elsewhere. It is written at large international conferences and by the UNESCO teams working so that the illiterate people of the world — and that means half of those alive today — may learn to read and write.

And it is a story being written by the educators of the member nations in their own countries. In the reports from the National Commissions sent to UNESCO House, over and over this appears: "Studying about the United Nations is now part of our regular school curriculum." Young people and children on every continent are today studying the Charter of the United Nations, which has been translated into many languages. They are studying the Declaration of Human Rights which most of them can read in their own language, for it, too, has been widely translated. They are studying the publications of the United Nations, of UNESCO, and of the other Specialized Agencies. It is the first time in history that so many students in schools and colleges around the world have had the *selfsame* texts and are reading the *selfsame* words.

In the United States, the roll call of classes learning about the United Nations is the roll call of schools in every state. Very few do not include study of the UN. In some cities, the teachers have drawn up special UN courses for each elementary school grade, each year of high school. In St. Paul, the elementary school UN curriculum plan is called *Let's Face the Facts and Act;* that for their high schools, *The United Nations: You and Others.* In New York City, the UN curriculum plan is *A Better World.* In it, even kindergarten children and those in the first and second grades have their UN activities. "Sharing toys and books fairly. Working pleasantly with others. Displaying kindness toward classmates. Finding pictures of children of our land and other lands." And the United States Office of Education has published *World Understanding Begins with Children,* by Delia Goetz.

Across the country, school assembly programs show UN films. They feature model General Assembly, Security Council, and Trusteeship Council meetings. In Detroit, after the students of nineteen high schools have studied about the UN for a semester, they have a joint General Assembly meeting. To be chosen to appear on it is a coveted honor. The audience demand for tickets always exceeds the number available. In hundreds of schools each year exhibits on the Declaration of Human Rights are set up — not so large nor so impressive, to be sure, as that arranged in Paris by UNESCO, in which man's age-old fight for freedom was dramatized for the delegates to its fourth General Conference, but with the same inner meaning.

Many French young people were among the crowds that thronged the Musée Galliéra where the Paris exhibition was held. There they saw the documents lent from the archives of various governments — documents which are landmarks in the peoples' fight for their human rights. From the United States, these documents included a rough draft of the Declaration of Independence in Thomas Jefferson's own handwriting, a reading copy of the Gettysburg Address autographed by Abraham Lincoln, and an original copy of the Bill of Rights.

So many exhibition visitors were so profoundly impressed by the dramatic photographs showing UN's work for a peace based on the Four Freedoms as stated by President Franklin D. Roosevelt in his famous message, that in answer to popular demand UNESCO later made an album of them for schools and organizations to use in their own Human Rights exhibitions and on their bulletin boards.

Another important part of UNESCO's work in schools has to do with the textbooks that young people and children are studying. Back in League of Nations days educators from various countries began meeting to discuss how textbooks could be written so that through them international understanding would be helped, not hindered.

"By the time I was a boy in Norway," an eminent Norwegian-American citizen said not long ago, "our educators and those in Sweden had awakened to the fact that what our boys and girls were being taught in our two countries was doing a lot of harm. Our textbooks played up the differences between us, especially the wars we had fought against each other. To be sure, we were different. We had fought those wars. But what we had done together was much more important.

"As I understand it, the Norwegian and Swedish educators got together on this. In any event, by the time I was a boy, our school textbooks had changed. One day I found my grandfather reading my history book. 'I wish I had had this book instead of the one I studied when I was your age,' he told me. 'Why?' I asked him. 'Because then I wouldn't be finding myself so antagonistic toward the Swedes every so often,' he said. 'I don't like to feel that way.' 'Then why do you?' I asked him. He smiled ruefully. 'It jumps back on me,' he replied, 'because I learned it when I was your age.'"

Such feelings are what Jaime Torres Bodet calls "traffic blocks in the mind," and UNESCO is working to clear away those blocks. Educators from many countries come together in large UNESCO conferences to talk about what can be done, as in Brussels, when they discussed textbooks of many kinds, and in Montreal, when their subject was *Geography in International Understanding*.

American teachers, meeting in their National Education Association and other organizations, are studying this same situation as regards the textbooks used in the United States. One state, Kansas, has a state-wide project on them, with high school students joining in the discussions. Under Milton D. Eisenhower, then President of Kansas State College of Agriculture and Applied Science and first chairman of the United States National Commission, Kansas started organizing itself for UNESCO. Today that organization is exceptional, with UNESCO groups in Kansas counties, cities, towns, and rural communities, and in youth and adult organizations.

Two of the questions that these UNESCO groups are asking in Kansas

are: "Do our textbooks contribute or fail to contribute to international understanding? Do they encourage prejudices against those who are different?"
If they do not contribute to international understanding, if they do encourage
prejudices, Kansas is prepared to do something about it, for the state pub-
lishes most of its own textbooks.

Such is the work of UNESCO as it brings together educators and scientists of many countries. Such are chapters from *The UNESCO Story*, published by the United States National Commission, all of it the stirring record
of the peoples speaking with the peoples.

When the members of the UNESCO Thinkers' Club in the East Senior
High School in Pawtucket, Rhode Island, wrote their club charter, they
took as their goal: "To learn everything we can about the Declaration of
Human Rights. To 'live' UNESCO thoughts. To be one in spirit with
UNESCO, trying to grow in knowledge and goodness." Youth speaking with
youth — and those memorable words in the Preamble to UNESCO's Constitution: "Since wars begin in the minds of men, it is in the minds of men that
the defenses of peace must be constructed."

RITCHIE CALDER SAW

MANY MEN OF THE DESERT WITH PRIMITIVE PLOWS SUCH AS THIS

HE HAS FOUND
A FASCINATING BOOK IN MUNICH'S
INTERNATIONAL YOUTH LIBRARY

WITHOUT BOUNDARIES It is exhibit day at

UNESCO House. There, for all visitors to enjoy, is displayed the work of a
group of young Egyptians. There are pictures they have painted, sculpture
they have modeled, tapestries they have woven. Those who come to the exhibition hall exclaim over the beauty created by the young artists, all of
whom are under twenty years of age. Who are they? Who made it possible
for them to do such exceptional work? Sayeda Missac could have told,
because her sculpture was there.

For Sayeda it had all begun years before in her Cairo schoolroom. She
did not see the visitor come in that morning. All her thoughts were on the
lump of clay in her hand. "Please God," she was whispering, "let me make
it *very* ferocious." For she had decided to model Daniel in the Lions' Den,
and never having seen a lion knew only that it must be *very* ferocious. As
the visitor, Habib Gorgi, afterward said, what Sayeda then created did not
look like a lion in the least, but it was indeed a most ferocious creature. And
in it, Mr. Gorgi saw the work of unusual young talent.

For many years, Habib Gorgi, chief inspector of art for the Egyptian

Ministry of Education, has been a friend of the young people and children of his country. He himself has taught art classes for them and has supervised many more. And some especially gifted children he has taken into his own home where, as he says, "We sit upon the floor and we work and sing together and are very happy." Soon after Sayeda modeled her very ferocious creature, she went to live with Mr. and Mrs. Gorgi. Modeling to her heart's content, she enjoyed watching her companions carve and weave and paint. And when those at UNESCO House heard about the remarkable work these young Egyptians were doing, they sent an invitation to Mr. Gorgi to have an exhibit of his pupils' work in Paris.

Not long after the Egyptian exhibition, twelve teen-age artists of six countries had their day at UNESCO House. Each picture on the walls was a poster design on the theme, "Together we build a better world." All had been painted by young people in their schools for UNESCO's poster and essay contest. On the opening day, the authors of the winning essays were announced, and the essays read. It was a truly international contest. The judges were from Brazil, China, France, India, Switzerland, and the United Kingdom. And the prize posters and essays were the work of teen-agers in Australia, Belgium, Denmark, India, Mexico, North Ireland, Scotland, South Africa, and Switzerland. These posters and essays, reproduced in *The Unesco Courier*, brought wide praise.

The young artists of the world, all young people who enjoy fine pictures, sculpture, and other beautiful things, have their place in UNESCO House, together with young musicians and lovers of music, and those interested in the dramatic arts. For UNESCO is working in many ways so that more people may have more of this beauty, as it has been created by the artists of many countries.

In order that those may do so who do not have the opportunity to see fine pictures, UNESCO's Art Committee has published a list of the best reproductions of the most beautiful paintings done from the year 1860 to the present. In this catalogue, which is called *Colour Reproductions*, information is given about where each reproduction may be obtained, in any part of the world. When the catalogue was completed, a reproductions exhibition was held at UNESCO House, and shortly similar traveling exhibits were on their way to Australia, Brazil, Ecuador, Haiti, Mexico, Norway, Peru, Tunisia, Uruguay, and the British African territories. There thousands of young people who live far from any art museum were among the many who came to see the pictures.

It is young composers' night at UNESCO House, and five young musicians are on the program to play their own compositions — Hectare Tosare of Uruguay, Karol Goeyvaerts of Belgium, Charles Jones of the United States, Narces Bonet of Spain, and Olivier Alain of France. All deeply appreciate the opportunity UNESCO has given them, for one of the greatest difficulties of composers everywhere is finding the chance to perform their work in public.

How did UNESCO hear about Hectare, Karol, Charles, and the others? Through the International Council of Music, which has brought together the musical organizations of the world and which UNESCO helped organize. The concerts for the "unknowns" were made possible by a gift from the International Music Fund, one of the Council's member organizations.

Like the Art Committee, the International Council of Music has many different plans, and UNESCO helps in carrying them out. When an orchestra came from the Union of South Africa to give concerts of native Afrikaans music in the United States, and at the same time an orchestra went from the United States to South Africa to play American music, it was because the Council arranged the exchange through the National Commissions of UNESCO in the two countries.

Teen-agers in various countries have started Junior Music groups because through UNESCO they heard about *Jeunesses Musicales*. Upward of ten years ago, M. Marcel Cuvelier, executive director of the Brussels Philharmonic Society and a member of the Council's executive board, started the *Jeunesses Musicales* for those between the ages of twelve and twenty-five who were young musicians or who loved music even though they themselves played no instrument. How they managed to keep on with their rehearsing during the occupation days of World War II is difficult to conceive, but they did. Today, in Brussels alone, more than ten thousand teen-agers belong to Junior Music. They have their own orchestra and choral society. They publish their own magazine with news about the theater and motion pictures as well as about musical events. They take over blocks of seats at concerts, selling them to Junior Music members at reduced prices, and carry on many other kinds of musical activity.

Each year, Junior Music holds an international congress, for its members are now to be found in Australia, Belgium, Denmark, India, Mexico, North Ireland, Scotland, South Africa, Switzerland, and elsewhere. One of the special events of every congress program is the symphony concert played by an orchestra whose musicians are young people from many countries.

For those whose special enthusiasm is for dramatic productions of any kind, there is the International Theatre Institute at UNESCO House. The Institute's members are organizations in many parts of the world who work together so that more people may have the beauty of the dramatic arts to enjoy. Through it, new national theaters have been organized in some countries, and the Institute is arousing interest for establishing more of them.

When International Theatre Month is celebrated around the world every March, with plays, pageants, and festivals, it is because the Institute has planned it. In the United States, more than four hundred dramatic groups take part in International Theatre Month, many of them high school dramatic clubs. Some produce plays laid in countries abroad and written by authors of nationalities other than American. Other groups give festivals originated especially for the occasion, such as *Voices of UNESCO — One Song — One Dance — One World,* staged by more than twelve hundred children of the York, Pennsylvania, schools. The members of the large caste — pupils from the first grade through the sixth — wore costumes of the member nations of UNESCO in the tableaux, songs, and dances of the festival. Whatever kind of International Theatre Month production is given, all are alike in that they contribute in some way to international understanding.

Beautiful art, music, dramatic productions — and books.

It is homecoming day in the young people's and children's room of the Public Library in the Hague. Everyone is excited, for any moment the door will open and there Miss Wolff will be once more. Miss Johanna Rebecca Wolff, their librarian who has been away for six months in the United States. What a trip she has had! From Cleveland, Ohio, to Washington, D.C.; to Chicago, Illinois; to Detroit and Kalamazoo in Michigan; to Pittsburgh, Pennsylvania; to Boston, Massachusetts; to Newark, New Jersey; to Albany and New York City in New York State; even up into Canada to Toronto. From each place, she sent them picture postcards. And now she has come back.

At last the door swings wide and there is their Miss Wolff. She is smiling joyfully, and her arms are so full of books she can scarcely keep her hold on

IT IS INTERNATIONAL THEATRE
MONTH, AND THIS MOUNT HOLYOKE
COLLEGE STUDENT IS BEING MADE UP
FOR HER PART IN A FRENCH PLAY

ST. PAUL, MINNESOTA,
CAMP FIRE GIRLS MADE THIS
TREASURE CHEST,
FILLED IT WITH NEW BOOKS,
AND NOW ARE DELIVERING
THEIR GIFT
TO THEIR PUBLIC LIBRARY
FOR SHIPMENT TO NORWAY

A UNESCO FELLOWSHIP
BROUGHT JOHANNA WOLFF,
YOUNG PEOPLE'S
AND CHILDREN'S LIBRARIAN
IN THE HAGUE,
TO THE UNITED STATES
AND THESE NEW FRIENDS
IN THE CLEVELAND
PUBLIC LIBRARY

them as the library teen-agers and children surge around her in welcome. Even before she can put the books down on one of the tables, they start in with their questions. Did she meet any American young people and children? What are they like?

"Of course I met them," Miss Wolff told her young Dutch friends. "What are they like? Well, I'll tell you. The first thing they all did was to take a quick look at my shoes. You should have seen the expression on their faces when they saw I wasn't wearing wooden ones! They were actually disappointed that mine were the same as theirs."

Miss Wolff's audience had a good laugh over that. What an idea, thinking that everyone in the Netherlands wears wooden shoes!

"But wait a minute," Miss Wolff went on quickly. "When one boy brought me a red feather, he said, 'This is for your boys. It is a real Indian feather from a chief's headdress my uncle gave me. But be sure to tell everybody at your library that not all Americans are Indians.'" Miss Wolff paused, then continued, "Do you know, in all the time I was in the United States, I didn't see a single Indian!"

The superiority on the faces of her audience vanished. One by one, they started to laugh, but it was a different kind of laughter. "You see!" cried Miss Wolff.

Then she plunged into her story. Everyone had been so friendly that from the day she arrived in the United States, she had felt right at home. "Once when I visited a classroom in one of the American schools, a small boy came up to me and stretching out his hand said, 'I am the host.' Then he took me around, explaining everything. The hospitality of that little boy is a wonderful example of the welcome everyone gave me in the beautiful children's rooms of the public libraries I visited and in the libraries of the schools. And the books!"

Yes, of course, the books. What do American teen-agers like to read? "Just what you do," Miss Wolff told them. "Some of their books are the same ones we have right here — *Treasure Island, Little Women, The Arabian Nights.* Like you, they can never get too many stories, adventure stories, horse stories — you know!"

Pausing, she searched among the books she had brought with her. "Here are some of the new stories that have just been published in the United States for teen-age readers. It's a good thing you are learning English at school, for you will be able to read these and the others."

The others? "Yes," Miss Wolff told them, "more are coming, a gift to you from our American friends who sent us the treasure chest of new books, right after the war."

Then those next younger than the teen-agers had their turn, with Miss Wolff telling them that over in America *Winnie-the-Pooh, Alice in Wonderland,* and *The Moffats* are every bit as popular as with the Hague library readers. And the picture books there on the table! How gay they were, with their pictures of adorable puppies and kittens and ponies, and small boys and girls.

As fascinating as the books was Miss Wolff's story of her visits to American library rooms for young readers. As she described them, her audience could fairly see them — the brightness of them, the low chairs and tables for the smallest children, the special corners, even the special rooms for the teen-agers. She had been to story hours and to book exhibits. She had taken part in Book Week, which is celebrated in every state in the United States once a year — yes, indeed, in every single state, with young library readers having book parties, giving book plays, marching in book parades.

"But there," said Miss Wolff, "I can't begin to tell you everything at one time. We'll look at the books now, and when next you come, I'll give you another chapter of my United States story."

Busy days followed for Johanna Rebecca Wolff, there in the Netherlands. She returned to teaching her classes in children's literature and library work for the Dutch children's and young people's librarians. She went out to teachers' and parents' groups to tell about her trip. And she visited city and town officials to make plans for starting new school libraries.

Miss Wolff's visit to the United States was made possible by a UNESCO fellowship. As with all applications for the fellowships awarded by UNESCO, hers was carefully considered at UNESCO House. There those whose work is with libraries and books saw by her papers that for more than ten years before World War II, Miss Wolff had been the children's and young people's librarian in the Hague Public Library, and a splendid one. But she had not stopped with work in her own library. She had gone into many parts of her country, interesting educators and parents in starting libraries in the schools. Her request for a UNESCO fellowship in the United States was made because she wished to learn just how American librarians are making their young people's and children's rooms so attractive and useful. She wished to study library methods at one of America's fine library schools. And she wished to become acquainted with librarians and teen-agers and children, alike.

When UNESCO granted a fellowship to Miss Wolff, those at the national headquarters of the American Library Association in Chicago made plans for her six months' stay. Mildred Batchelder, who is in charge of young people's and children's work for the Association, worked out her itinerary. Cleveland was chosen as her headquarters, and Jean Roos, head of the Cleveland Public Library's Robert Louis Stevenson Room for young people, and Elizabeth Briggs, director of children's work, were appointed special hostesses. For the library courses Miss Wolff wished to study, she was to go to the Library School of Western Reserve University. Plenty of time was allowed for her to get acquainted with the teen-agers and children of Cleveland. And she would visit many more libraries, meet many more librarians and young readers as she traveled to other cities. She was also to visit the Office of Education in Washington to see what the United States Government is doing for libraries and there to talk with Nora Beust, specialist for school and children's libraries.

All the plans worked out splendidly — a dream come true for Johanna Rebecca Wolff. But the giving was not one-sided. Many teen-agers in the American libraries Miss Wolff visited have a warm, happy memory of her hours with them and of what she told about her friends in Holland.

More libraries — many people in many parts of the world are eager for them and UNESCO is helping to start them. Librarians from countries that have had libraries for a long time, those of the International Federation of Library Associations meet to help plan UNESCO booklets and bulletins in which are suggestions for organizing and carrying on all kinds of libraries. School officials, those in the town, city, or national government departments of any of UNESCO's member nations, can — and do — find at UNESCO House the library help they need.

UNESCO also sponsors special libraries in various parts of the world. One of these is the International Youth Library in Munich. There, as in the Children's Library at the League of Nations building in Geneva, books for young readers are gathered together from around the world. Many friends worked to make possible the Munich plan which was originated by Mrs. Jella

Lepman: the Bavarian Government that remodeled for its use a charming three-story *schloss;* the Friends of the Library Committee whose members included a representative of the Bavarian *Kulturministerium;* the Munich Superintendent of Schools; head librarians of the Munich Public Library and of the State Library; the Chief of the Bavarian Youth Bureau; and a member of the Bavarian Radio Station. They and other interested German citizens helped raise the money necessary to match that granted the Library by the Rockefeller Foundation.

When the International Youth Library was opened, among the guests was Margaret C. Scoggin, Young People's Specialist in the New York Public Library and chairman of the American Library Association's International Relations Committee. "Even more interesting to me than the adult committees," wrote Miss Scoggin for *The Horn Book* magazine, "was the committee of some thirty young people representing Munich secondary schools, which met a month or so before opening day to hear about the library and make plans for their part in it. Thanks to the voluntary aid of many of this group, the books for the library were unpacked, recorded, and prepared in time for the opening. It is this group which has since formed the nucleus for book discussion, book reviewing, preparation of exhibits, and discussion of policies.

"The library opened with an exhibit of children's paintings from some twenty-two countries and an exhibit of children's books from twenty-three countries. I wish I could describe in technicolor all the preparations made at the last minute: the gay geraniums and marigolds planted along the entrance way the evening before by a corps of gardeners; the waxing and polishing of everything from stairways to doorstep by the devoted *Putzfrau;* the rearrangement of the gay paintings; the search by the young committee members for just the right page of each book for display.

"I wish I could reproduce for you with sound effects the appealing program in which boys and girls from several lands read bits in their own tongues from their favorite children's books — *Pinocchio, Babar, Ferdinand, Emil and the Detectives, Heidi, The Wonderful Adventures of Nils* — and concluded by singing a round, 'Are you sleeping?' in English, French, German, and Swedish!

"In the afternoon our Fritz, seventeen-year-old member of the young people's committee, took over as master of ceremonies for the children's party. He wrote his own speech and delivered it with sincerity. Among other things, he said:

" 'The International Youth Library has opened for us our first window on the world and has brought us a step nearer to Germany's inclusion again in the circle of nations. It gives us a chance to busy ourselves freely with the thoughts of the whole world. I hope it will also help us make personal contacts with young people of other lands and show us that there are many peace-loving people and that understanding among such people is possible.

" 'We ourselves will do our best to win friends for the International Youth Library. And this one thing we will never forget: for the young people of other countries, we young people here will always be a little mirror of our own people. We want to show the world that we Germans are capable of working peacefully with other peoples. And we must all together help toward that.' "

But what are libraries without books? More books for more people — this, too, is part of UNESCO's work. As soon as UNESCO was organized, it started its plans for more books around the world. At once, it came up against book traffic blocks.

One of these traffic blocks has to do with the customs charges made when books are sent from one country to another. In some places, these charges are so high that when they are added to the cost of a book, its original price is trebled. This makes books so expensive that in many places the people cannot afford to buy them at all. In others, even where the people purchase books, the number they can obtain for their money is small compared to what they wish to buy.

By vote of its General Conference, UNESCO has been working so that books, works of art, films, and other educational materials may be sent from one country to another without any customs charges. In order to bring this about, it is necessary for a sufficient number of the member governments to agree to it. Already, some have done so. Others are considering the plan and are favorably inclined to it. Sending books free across national boundaries is a not impossible goal.

UNESCO has built a detour around another book traffic block. This block has to do with the two kinds of money in the world — the "soft currency" and the "hard currency." Before UNESCO built the detour, those in the soft-currency countries could not send a money order or a check for books to the hard-currency countries, because the booksellers in the hard-currency countries could not cash the money order or the check.

What UNESCO did about this situation has been called by Luther H. Evans, Librarian of Congress, "an outstanding example of UNESCO's practical approach in overcoming one of the toughest obstacles to the free flow of information between peoples."

Today if the young members of a Science Club in Persia, which has soft currency, have the money for a science book published in the United States, all they need to do is to buy a UNESCO book coupon with their own money, sending the coupon to America with their order. The bookseller in the United States will accept the coupon in payment because he knows he can get his American money by presenting the coupon to the American Bookseller's Association, the organization in the United States with whom UNESCO worked out the plan. This is UNESCO's book coupon procedure, the detour over which many books have already traveled.

To other hard-currency countries UNESCO is offering the same kind of arrangement, working with organizations similar to the American Bookseller's Association. As a result, more and more hard-currency countries are joining in as booksellers and more and more soft-currency countries are using the coupons for their book purchases.

UNESCO also has a gift plan by which schools, Boy Scout and Girl Scout troops, and other groups may buy book coupons for the classes and schools in other countries in which they are interested. Coupons for as little as twenty-five cents may be bought, and held until there is ten dollars' worth of them. Then the ten-dollar coupon is sent abroad, and the school or class there uses it to buy the books for which they have been wishing.

More books for more people — but what if you are blind? What UNESCO has done for books for the blind is an outstanding achievement. Years ago, Louis Braille, himself a blind man, devised the alphabet of raised dots that bears his name. In the years following the first Braille book, the system spread around the world. But as it spread, it was changed to fit the different languages. The result was that in time there were more than twenty-five separate Braille systems, and Braille books could not be widely exchanged. This was a great pity, since because of it many blind boys and girls were without books to read which otherwise they might have had.

Among those called to UNESCO House to discuss this unfortunate situation was Sir Clutha MacKenzie of New Zealand, who, blinded in World War I, has since devoted his life to those similarly handicapped. "We must work out one system of Braille for everyone, no matter what his language," Sir Clutha declared.

One system of Braille script for all languages — it would seem an impossible plan. Yet it is being accomplished. Experts from many countries have held meeting after meeting to grapple with the intricacies of the various languages. It has taken international co-operation, too. It was not easy for those to change whose peoples have for centuries been reading from right to left. But for the sake of blind people everywhere, they have agreed that Braille will now be read from left to right around the world.

When the announcement of this achievement was made at an International Braille Conference at UNESCO House, Helen Keller said, "Through your work a new era for the blind is beginning, lifting the blind throughout the world into the light of culture and knowledge."

And Sir Clutha said, "In this one way, we who are blind will shortly be a step ahead of sighted people. We shall have a universal script."

More books for more people — but what if you have never learned to read?

Leaning back against the clay wall, staring dully at the sun-baked ground outside, Ti-Joseph and Gésila sat on the dirt floor of the one-room shack that was their home. On a frayed straw mat in the corner, their father lay sick. Beside him, their mother listlessly tried to keep the flies from him and the baby in her arms. Listlessly and hopelessly, for there was despair in her heart. Two days ago, they had started eating their seed corn. When that was gone, there would be nothing, for there was no money with which to buy even a small bit of millet bread or rice, even one mango from the peddler at his roadside stand in the valley below. No money — and no food except the corn.

Her husband stirred restlessly, and she laid a comforting hand upon his forehead. It was not his fault that each year life became more difficult than ever before. Every day that he was not sick, he took his hoe and his machete and scrambling up the slope of the mountain, worked in the clearing that was their only hope for food. When Ti-Joseph went along to help, as he often

GESILA
BEAT TI-JOSEPH
IN LEARNING
TO READ

LIKE THE OTHERS IN THE MARBIAL VALLEY,
GESILA AND TI-JOSEPH LIVED IN A
ONE-ROOM, STRAW-THATCHED SHACK

THE LUCKY FAMILY
TO MOVE INTO THIS MODEL HOME,
BUILT BY THE UN TEAM,
FOUND IT MUCH MORE COMFORTABLE
THAN THEIR OLD ONE

THE MARBIAL VALLEY
PEOPLE WERE GRATEFUL TO
THEIR NEW FRIENDS FOR
SHOWING THEM HOW TO
MAKE CRAFT ARTICLES
THAT WOULD SELL

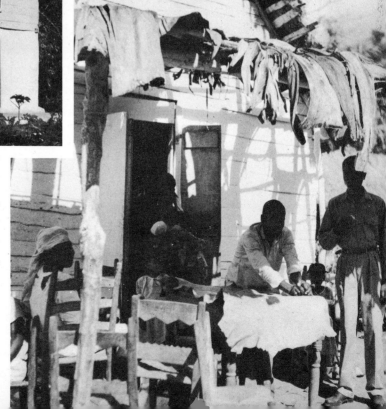

did, his father tied him to a tree with a long rope lest some misstep send him crashing down the mountainside. A fifteen-year-old is not so careful as his father.

Soon the ground on the slope would become as poor as that near their shack. Perhaps even more so because the rains of the wet season washed the good topsoil down into the river below. Each year, less good soil. Each year, less food for the family. And they never knew when a long drought would come — as now.

Along the dry and rocky bed of the river called Gosseline, in the valley below Ti-Joseph's and Gésila's shack home, a car was wending its jolting way toward them. In it were the members of a UNESCO team, come to see what could be done to make life better for the twenty-six thousand men and women, young people and children, who lived there in the Marbial Valley of Haiti.

Much had happened in Haiti before the car, bumping over the rocks, could start out. Upward of a year earlier, a UN mission had gone to Haiti, a large mission whose members were experts from many parts of the United Nations. These experts, joining those of Haiti, had studied the entire country — its agriculture, its industries, its schools, and much else — and their suggestions for Haiti's future had been published in a UN book called *Mission to Haiti*.

When representatives of the Haitian Government then went to UNESCO to ask for its special help in the Marbial Valley, those at UNESCO House studied the report of the UN mission. The invitation itself was discussed by UNESCO's executive board and by its General Conference. And when, at length, it was decided to accept, the UNESCO-Haiti Government partnership for the valley was given a special name, that of Pilot Project. *Pilot* because what was done there, what the UNESCO workers would learn, would be a guide to UNESCO itself for other projects in other underdeveloped areas around the world.

There was no doubt that the Marbial Valley was underdeveloped. Ninety per cent of its people could not read or write. For many years, they had so mistreated the soil that the only way they could continue to make anything grow was to cut down trees on the mountain slopes and use the newly cleared land there. The fallen trees they made into charcoal for the outdoor fireplaces where they cooked their meals. But they did not plant more trees. The topsoil on the slopes, no longer held in place by tree roots, was washed away during each wet season. Ti-Joseph's mother was right. Every year less food was grown in the valley.

There was a great deal of sickness among the Marbial people — malaria from mosquitoes breeding in the Gosseline's stagnant pools; yaws because of unsanitary conditions in the homes; hookworm and other diseases. The water everyone drank came from the river where cattle stood throughout the day and where the valley people themselves bathed. There was no doctor, no public health nurse. As for schools, only a few were to be found in the valley, and most of the young people and the children did not bother to attend them.

The Marbial Valley, Haiti — and now a UNESCO-government team was there. Dr. Alfred Metraux, distinguished anthropologist of UNESCO's Secretariat, was head of the team, most of whose members were Haitians. It was agreed that their first work would be to get acquainted with the Marbial Valley people, to study their educational needs, and to make a detailed, careful plan of action covering a period of years.

They found the people starving. Before the team did anything else, it set up feeding centers for the children and teen-agers. And one team member flew to the United States for the seed of quick-growing corn.

Two years have passed in the Marbial Valley. In front of a simple, charming building designed by a young Haitian architect, children are dancing in the final number of an afternoon's program. When they finish, the teen-agers and the men and women have their turn, whirling in their folk dances until late evening. Among those watching the festivities are workers from WHO as well as from UNESCO and the Haitian Government.

Since early morning they have been celebrating the opening of their new clinic, their Marbial Valley clinic. The dancing peasants do not know just what all the new equipment in the clinic is for, but they are certain that with it the doctor and the nurses will be able to help them even more than they have been doing in the old, crowded clinic room. And that is saying a great deal, for the doctor and the nurses have already done much. Who would have thought that liquid from a needle would cure the yaws? But it has done so.

There have been other celebrations during the two years just past, not all with special programs, but celebrations even so. There was the celebration for the new well, which the peasants helped dig and from which they now have good water to drink. When their new friends explained to them about good water and bad, they went to work with right good will. There was the celebration when their Community Center was finished, which they had helped build. Every day, now, something interesting was going on at the Center. It was there they saw the motion picture about hookworm, a film made by a man called Mr. Walt Disney, and so came to understand what a latrine is for and why there is not so much sickness when one is used. Already there are fifty latrine pits in the valley, and more are on the way.

There was their celebration for the model house which showed them how to build more comfortable homes; that for their seedling nursery from which they got the sturdy plants for the beans and the corn and the eggplant now growing in their gardens. There was their new market. And the road — the peasants were especially proud of that road. No longer would they be shut off from Jacmel, the nearest town, when, throughout the rainy season, the Gosseline's river bed was flooded. For generations, that river bed had been their only road.

They had refused to take any pay for their work on the road. And when the first stretch was finished, they had a parade, with signs printed by those who could write. *Kebe l'Inesko fo,* the signs said — *Support UNESCO Hard.*

In the hearts of those dancing in front of the new clinic, there was thankfulness for the new friends who had come to them, teaching them so many good things. They understood now why it was important to keep their homes and themselves clean. They were grateful for the new tools, a great deal better than their old ones. Plowing the furrows in circles on the mountain slopes was a good idea, too. The rains did not wash so much soil away as when the furrows went straight up and down.

What they learned in the new school made sense. All went there, grown men and women as well as those younger. For the women and girls, sewing and cooking lessons were among the classes held. The men and boys learned such things as how to care for your animals — your ox, for instance. All were taught how to take care of the soil, how to cultivate what was planted.

One thing led to another with these new friends, it seemed. The sisal that the men were now planting on the slopes and which helped hold the soil in place had fibers that could be braided, then woven into mats. And the merchants in Jacmel were buying the mats. They were also buying other things that the people were making in their homes, the leatherwork and the rope.

It was good just to be in the schoolroom with its bright pictures on the walls and its music. That was another magic, music coming from a platter on a machine! It was fun to listen to and fun to dance to after their lessons were over. The games were fun, too, especially the one with the large ball and the net, which was called volley ball.

And the books! Everyone was enchanted with them. Written in their own Creole language, the books, too, made sense. In them you learned many things that you could use every day. They had every right to be proud of those books, their UNESCO friends said, for they had been written especially for those of Haiti by their own people in Port-au-Prince. The pictures in them had been drawn and painted by Haitian artists. To help them, a man who knew a great deal about books had come all the way from UNESCO House in Paris. And their government had printed them so that they, the people of the Marbial Valley, would no longer remain in ignorance.

It was the peasants' way of expressing what a UNESCO official had said: "Books have been turned into weapons of survival."

Learning to read had been exciting. Ti-Joseph and Gésila had had a race with their mother and father over who would first be able to do it. It did not take long, what with the charts filled with pictures. And Gésila won.

It had not been necessary to go to school for the reading lessons. Throughout the valley, in little banana-leaf shelters, teen-agers and children, grown men and women had met with their teachers. As soon as anyone learned to read, he helped someone else. Even those as young as six or seven were to be seen pointing out letters or words to their mothers and fathers there in the shelters.

The books so welcome to young and old in the Marbial Valley, that have been so helpful to them, are part of UNESCO's international campaign against illiteracy. In this campaign UNESCO faces a tremendous task. Half the people of the world cannot read and write. Yet only when they are able to do so can they take their place in the modern world. Only then can they know what is happening and what it means. Only then will they be able to communicate with those of other countries, to meet them in understanding and live with them in peace.

To achieve this task, UNESCO calls together large and small conferences of educators from many countries to discuss the best ways of teaching reading and writing. Among those who have come to these meetings are men and women of long and valuable experience in the same work in their own countries, such as Jaime Torres Bodet who, as Minister of Education in Mexico, directed a campaign through which in two years one million, two hundred thousand of the Mexican people learned to read and write.

As these educators decide just how to proceed in UNESCO's literacy campaign, the work done in times past by others in distant parts of the world is a helpful guide to them. Just how did the great pioneer, Frank C. Laubach, succeed in teaching so many to read and write, and that quickly, first among the Moro people of the Philippines, where he was a missionary, then among other peoples to whom he went throughout the Far East? The books, the charts that he and other pioneers have developed, for beginning readers of whatever age, are important to UNESCO and there is a collection of them at UNESCO House. Also in the collection are the new books, charts, and films that UNESCO's educators have more recently prepared. All are at the service of the Departments of Education of the member nations.

And the member nations use them. When seven-year-old Ram Chandra and his thirty-five-year-old father sat down side by side for their reading lesson in the little town of Adilabad in rural India, the book in their hands had been prepared by their UNESCO-government friends. And their teacher's charts were from those selfsame friends.

As the young people, the children, the men, and the women of the Marbial Valley go into the fields, to their clinic, their Community Center, their market, and their school, those at UNESCO House are studying what has been accomplished among them. That which is being carried out there, UNESCO's partnership with FAO and WHO, has its own name — Fundamental Education, which is education for better living in every way. And Fundamental Education is being used in the plans of the United Nations and the governments for underdeveloped areas around the world.

What, then, of the Marbial Valley? Have all the people there learned well what the partnership team has taught them? No, not all, for in no group

FROM THIS UNITED NATIONS
HEADQUARTERS IN JOGJAKARTA,
INDONESIA, THE TEAMS WENT OUT
TO TEACH AND TO LEARN

JOGJAKARTA BOYS
BECAME EXPERTS
IN CLEANING
THE CENTER'S
EQUIPMENT

JOGJAKARTA GIRLS LEARNED
TO PREPARE MILK WITH POWDER
AND WATER, OVER A CHARCOAL FIRE

THE DRIVER, DELIVERING SUPPLIES
WITH HER THREE-WHEEL INDONESIAN
CONVEYANCE, KNEW SHE WAS A
MEMBER OF A UNITED NATIONS TEAM

of people anywhere does that happen. But many have learned, are learning. More and more of the men are becoming better farmers; more and more of the women, better homemakers. More of the young people and children are going to school. More adults are attending their own classes. More of all the valley's people are healthier and happier.

Can the soil be made to yield enough food for everyone who lives in the valley? That is the question which remains to be answered, that is the goal which must be reached. For while the amount of food now being raised in the Marbial Valley has increased somewhat over the yield of the days before the UNESCO team arrived, nevertheless, the total crop still falls short of what the people need for good health. And grave difficulties stand in the way of the UNESCO-WHO-government partners, as they consult with the experts of FAO about next steps and about a long-range plan for the future.

Yet even the difficulties are a guide to the United Nations partners. Since the day the United Nations Charter was signed in San Francisco, the peoples have worked and learned together in new ways. Men and women have learned. Young people and children have learned. The teams have learned; the doctor at his lonely post; the nurse guiding her jeep through the jungle. Those in the fields, in their homes, and in their schools have learned; those in laboratories and on ships upon the sea; in stores, in factories, in banks. Governments have learned, in cities, in towns, in villages.

All have learned, and through their learning, the United Nations itself has learned. In the days to come, that learning will be its strength. For through that which has been done, the peoples have grown closer to one another in understanding, the youth of the world among them.

Youth, today and tomorrow, and a world in which the Declaration of Human Rights becomes an ever more living reality.

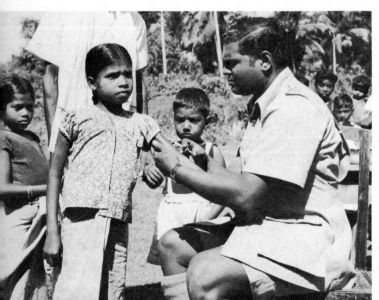

SINCE THE DAY
THE UNITED NATIONS
CHARTER WAS SIGNED,
THE PEOPLES
HAVE LEARNED TOGETHER,
THIS NATIVE DOCTOR
IN KAMATAWATTE, CEYLON,
AND HIS PATIENTS
AMONG THEM —

— TOGETHER THIS
GREEK DOCTOR AND HIS TERAI,
INDIA, FRIENDS HAVE LEARNED

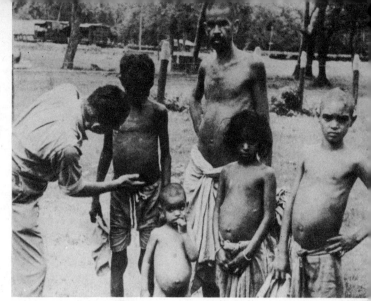

— THESE MALNAD,
INDIA, GIRLS,
WITH THEIR
TOOTHBRUSHES
MADE FROM TWIGS
AND THEIR
POWDERED CHARCOAL
TOOTH POWDER,
HAVE LEARNED,
AND SO HAS
THEIR TEACHER

— THIS TEEN-AGE HELPER
OF THE WHO BABY NURSE
IN DELHI, INDIA, HAS LEARNED

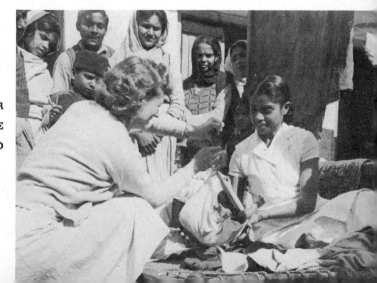

MANY PEOPLE, YOUNG AND OLD,
NEED HELP BEFORE THEY CAN START
THEIR UPWARD CLIMB

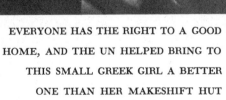

EVERYONE HAS THE RIGHT TO BE
FREE FROM FEAR, YET
UNTIL HIS UN FRIENDS
CAME, THIS WAR-ORPHANED BOY
WAS ALWAYS AFRAID

EVERYONE HAS THE RIGHT TO A GOOD
HOME, AND THE UN HELPED BRING TO
THIS SMALL GREEK GIRL A BETTER
ONE THAN HER MAKESHIFT HUT

HUMAN RIGHTS
Many of you young people probably wonder why the United Nations should pay so much attention to human rights. The real reason, of course, is that this is a subject which has been discussed down through the ages. Men have been struggling since the earliest days not only for existence, but also for certain human rights and fundamental freedoms. If in the United Nations we can get joint agreement among various nations to observe certain fundamental human rights and freedoms, and gradually come to a mutual understanding of what we mean when we talk about these rights and freedoms, we shall probably have laid a good cornerstone on which we may eventually be able to build a peaceful world.

War is a violation of human rights and freedoms. Once two or more nations are at war none of the people in these nations have any freedoms any more because the nation requires of them, if necessary, one of the most precious of human rights, the right to life.

The Human Rights Commission of the United Nations, when it sits down around the table, represents South and Central America, the United

States, the Far East, Europe, and the Middle East. It is easy to imagine that the delegate, for instance, from Denmark, the member from the Scandinavian countries, is more advanced in his approach toward human rights than some from other nations, because it has been traditional with Denmark and the other Scandinavian countries to believe in and fight for individual human rights and freedoms.

The Latin Americans, as a rule, recall their great liberator, Bolivar, who, to them, represents the fight to achieve freedom for human beings from one man or totalitarian rule. They are very conscious of human rights and freedoms but frequently have not as yet been able to realize them because of undeveloped conditions within their countries.

So far as the USSR and other totalitarian states go, naturally their interest lies in what the few men at the top consider fundamental for all people; namely, the improvement of their economic and social conditions. But any of the other equally important fundamental human rights, which actually emphasize the dignity of man as a thinking human being, do not seem very important to totalitarian nations.

There are some countries who frankly have never really thought of giving the mass of the people political freedom and therefore they have never given them sufficient education to handle that type of freedom. Some of these countries are found in the Middle East and Africa.

As you look at the whole Commission, you see a panorama of the world and human rights, and freedoms fit into that picture largely according to the development of the country agriculturally, industrially, and intellectually. The people sitting on the Commission, however, try to look at all the questions coming up before them as those questions affect all the different parts of the world, and to see the picture of the growth of understanding as it can be achieved everywhere.

This is the real reason for the concern in the United Nations about this particular question. It explains why the Economic and Social Council appointed a Commission of Human Rights to try to write a bill, not covering one people only, but covering all the people of the world. It was an effort to set down in words our joint agreement as to what are human rights and freedoms.

The Commission decided it would write first a declaration, somewhat like our own Declaration of Independence in the United States. This Declaration would voice rights already recognized in many countries as well as the desires of people even if in some cases it did not seem possible to attain them immediately. This would be followed by covenants or treaties where little by little these rights and freedoms would be set down in legal form. When a treaty is written, nations, according to the ways they have set up, ratify that treaty, and, having ratified it, they are bound to change their laws and live up to what they have agreed to do under the treaty.

Only the first of these treaties has been written. It covers some of the civil and political rights which we have had for a long time in this country and spells out how they are to be protected under the law. There is one important clause which says that every citizen shall enjoy these rights and freedoms regardless of race or creed or color.

Now let us go from what the Human Rights Commission is doing today back into history and see how we have come to our present situation.

The first preoccupation of man, of course, was to have some kind of shelter from the weather and to be able to get enough to eat. That provided existence, but very soon he began to feel there was something more than that which he wanted in life. He was not willing just to exist. He wanted to live. He developed the capacity to create things that made life pleasanter. He learned to make himself understood first through pictures and then through the written word. As he obtained greater skills, he realized that he needed certain rights and freedoms to protect his ability to live and that he should set them down in writing and have them accepted by what existed as a government for him, the head of a tribe, the head of a clan, or the head of a state.

One of the great landmarks not only in setting down these rights and freedoms, but in getting them accepted, was the English Magna Charta, which was signed by King John at Runnymede in 1215. This document granted to the people of England the legal right to a trial by jury of one's peers as well as certain other legal safeguards for the individual and his property.

Our own Declaration of Independence was adopted July 4, 1776, in Philadelphia. Our early American ancestors were very sure that their rights as human beings were being violated, and that is why they stated in the Preamble: "We hold these truths to be self-evident, that all men are created equal, that they are endowed by their Creator with certain unalienable

Rights, that among these are Life, Liberty and the pursuit of Happiness. That to secure these rights, Governments are instituted among Men, deriving their just powers from the consent of the governed . . . "

Our Declaration of Independence was followed in France by the Declaration of the Rights of Man, first adopted in 1789 during the French Revolution by the National Assembly of France, and later added to the first Republican Constitution of France in 1793. This recognized certain sacred rights, as, for example, political liberty, equality, freedom of speech and of religious worship, and certain safeguards in case of arrest and in criminal proceedings.

From these declarations which were studied by the great men of different periods, we come in our own history to another pronouncement made by Abraham Lincoln. He was talking about the authors of our Declaration of Independence and he said: "They did not mean to assert the obvious untruth that all men were then actually enjoying that equality, or yet that they were about to confer it immediately upon them. In fact, they had no power to confer such a boon. They meant simply to declare the *right* so that the enforcement of it might follow as soon as circumstances might permit."

That, as stated by Lincoln, is very much what we in the United Nations are trying to do today for the world as a whole. You will remember that Abraham Lincoln moved beyond just talking about human rights. It is told of him that long before he was President of the United States, at the sight of a slave, he asserted that if he ever got the chance to do something about slavery he would strike hard.

On New Year's Day, 1863, during the Civil War, Lincoln announced his Emancipation Declaration which ordered slaves in certain designated states henceforth to be free, and everyone remembers Lincoln's great Gettysburg address in which he said: "Fourscore and seven years ago our fathers brought forth on this continent a new nation, conceived in liberty and dedicated to the proposition that all men are created equal. . . . It is for us the living . . . to be dedicated here to the unfinished work which they who fought here have thus far so nobly advanced. . . . That this nation, under God, shall have a new birth of freedom — and that government of the people, by the people, for the people, shall not perish from the earth."

EVERYONE HAS THE RIGHT TO ENOUGH FOOD
— IT WAS THEIR UNICEF-GOVERNMENT FRIENDS WHO GAVE THESE
INDIAN GIRLS IN GUATEMALA THIS NOURISHING MILK

EVERYONE HAS THE
RIGHT TO AN EDUCATION
— AND PEPINO ALOJA,
AGREEING,
TOOK TIME OUT
FROM HIS LAW STUDIES
TO TEACH THE BOYS
OF NOVI VELIA VILLAGE
IN ITALY,
AFTER THE WAR
HAD WRECKED
THEIR ONLY SCHOOL

As a result of the Civil War, the Thirteenth, Fourteenth, and Fifteenth Amendments were added to the Constitution of the United States and this Constitution is the law of the land. Before these three Amendments were added, almost immediately after the Constitution had been written and adopted in 1788, there had been added twelve far-reaching Amendments. The first ten of these are frequently referred to as the American Bill of Rights and they were added to the Constitution in 1791. They guarantee, for example, the right known as habeas corpus, which is a legal remedy for determining when a person is illegally detained. They prohibit making some act a crime which was not a crime when it was committed. This is known as ex post facto law. They provide safeguards with respect to the fair conduct of trials. They contain provisions with regard to freedom of religion, of speech, and of the press, and provide for the right of trial by jury and the right peaceably to assemble and to petition the government for redress of grievances.

When the Thirteenth Amendment was added to the Constitution, slavery and involuntary servitude, except as punishment for crime, was prohibited. The Fourteenth Amendment prohibits states from depriving a person of life, liberty, or property without due process of law, or denying the equal protection of the law. The Fifteenth Amendment provides that the right of citizens of the United States to vote shall not be denied or abridged by the United States or by any state on account of race, color, or previous condition of servitude.

Years later, in 1919, we added the Nineteenth Amendment to the Constitution, which provides that the right of citizens to vote shall not be denied or abridged by the United States or by any state on account of sex. This Amendment is usually referred to as the Women's Suffrage Amendment.

In our country, in addition to our Federal Constitution, the states of the Union by their constitutions guarantee the people's rights and freedoms in numerous ways.

We see, therefore, that in the United States we have a long record in the matter of the preservation of human rights. Unfortunately many people take these rights for granted. They feel that because they are written down or assured in some document or some constitution, or by some law, they do not actually need to practice the right to vote, or their freedom to assemble or to associate, or their right to join community projects to better the life of the community, or their right to participate in activities aimed at preserving freedom to worship. In short, they do not feel that they have to do anything today about these numerous rights and freedoms which we have mentioned.

We have to understand that it is one thing to write things into the law but quite another thing for people to live up to the spirit of that law in their daily lives. Right here in our own country, in spite of the things we guarantee in the Amendments to the Constitution, we do not always find them lived up to by individual citizens. There are still many instances where it is difficult fully to enjoy fundamental human rights and freedoms even in the United States, and we probably grant in our country as many rights and freedoms to human beings as do some other countries of the world. Undoubtedly we grant more than do some countries. That is why even though we are a rather young country, we must take stock of ourselves very often to keep up our high standards of human rights and freedoms because only in this way can we live full lives. Only in this way can we be an example to be followed by other nations that have not thought so much as we have in the past about these fundamental rights and freedoms.

It is interesting to find that in San Francisco in 1945, when the United Nations Charter was drafted, the delegates put in seven references to human rights in the Charter. Article Fifty-five provides that the United Nations shall: "promote . . . universal respect for, and observance of, human rights for all without distinction as to race, sex, language, or religion." Article Fifty-six provides that all Members of the United Nations pledge themselves to take joint and separate action in co-operation with the Organization for the achievement of these purposes.

There are certain human rights which have been accepted over the years by quite a number of people, such, for instance, as freedom of religion. That means that you and I have the right to believe whatever we feel is true and that no one has a right to interfere with our convictions.

There are other well-recognized rights, such as the right of people to associate together and discuss their beliefs openly and peacefully. No one has a right, for instance, to advocate force, but people have the right to differ as to the way their government is administered and to say so, and they have the right to try to persuade other people to agree with them. This right of association implies also the right to freedom of speech and thought, and in our laws and in the laws of many lands the methods of protecting these rights have long been accepted.

People have a right to take part in their government. The reason that we felt so strongly against the Nazi Government and feel strongly today against any form of totalitarian government, is that people do not have the right openly to differ with the government in certain countries even in a peaceful manner.

Of late people have come to realize that there are certain social and economic rights which should be joined to the old traditional civil and political rights because if you are starving to death you may care very little about your right to take part in the government. Totalitarian states are apt to emphasize these social and economic rights above any others because the exercise of these rights does not require the same type of freedom of thought and action which must be present in real freedom of political activity and real freedom of expression, association, and worship.

The Four Freedoms as enunciated in the Atlantic Charter embrace most of the other human rights and freedoms. If you can be free from fear of aggression and free from fear of want and have freedom of worship, which means freedom of conscience and thought, and freedom of speech and expression, then you have actually achieved all the objectives of the United Nations Charter and the Declaration and first Covenant of Human Rights. Nevertheless, these rights have to be written down in order to put very clearly before people in a detailed way just what was in the minds of the men who wrote the Atlantic Charter and the United Nations Charter.

These documents are a guide for you and for me for our own conduct, and we should use them to check our actions day by day. We should be sure that we are not tolerating any abuses but in our lives are upholding the ideal of democracy which is based on justice that springs from the recognition and observance of the fundamental human rights and freedoms for all men regardless of race or creed or color.

IN APPRECIATION,
BIBLIOGRAPHY, AND INDEX

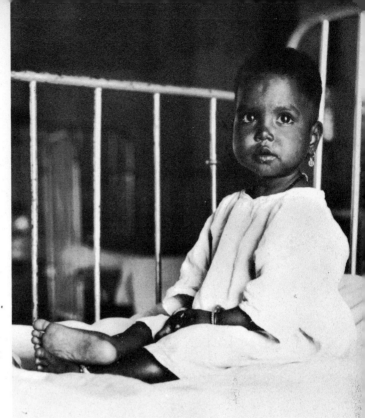

MEDICINE FROM
A UN TEAM IS HELPING HIM
GET WELL AT THE CHILDREN'S
HOSPITAL IN MADRAS, INDIA

IN APPRECIATION Many shared in the making of
this book, including members of the United Nations Secretariat who tirelessly searched files, records, and reports for stories and other material, and
the photographers who took the pictures in countries far and near. To them
all comes our deepest appreciation. We are especially indebted to:

BENJAMIN COHEN   United Nations Assistant Secretary-General for Public Information

RUTH CRAWFORD   Chief of Publications, the United Nations International Children's Emergency Fund

KAY RAINEY GRAY   Special research assistant for this book

MARGARET LESSER   Editor, Junior Books, Doubleday & Company, Inc.

GEORGE D. STODDARD   Chairman, the United States National Commission for UNESCO,
Department of State, and President of the University of Illinois

ALBERT B. TIBBETS   President, North Salem, New York, Free Library

We are also deeply grateful to the following whose help has been most
generous:

IT WAS A HAPPY WASHDAY WHEN UNICEF SOAP ARRIVED

IN THE UNITED NATIONS, DEPARTMENT OF PUBLIC INFORMATION   George J. Janecek, Chief Executive Officer. *External Services:* V. J. G. Stavridi, Director; Paul V. Johansen, Deputy Director in charge of liaison with Specialized Agencies; Mrs. Felice Lee, Liaison Officer for Specialized Agencies. *Central Editorial Services:* Leonard A. Berry, Chief. *Headquarters Services:* William Agar, Chief; Jane Weidlund, Assistant. *Film Section:* George Allen, Photographic Librarian; M. A. Weill, Assistant Photographic Librarian. *Radio Division:* Michael Hayward, Program Officer. *Library Services:* Mrs. Sonia Gruen, Security Council Affairs Departmental Librarian.

IN THE SPECIALIZED AGENCIES   *Food and Agriculture Organization:* Florence Reynolds, Chief, Public Information Branch. *International Refugee Organization:* Michael Wilson, Assistant Director, Office of Public Information; George R. Rowen, Public Information Officer. In the United States office of IRO, Washington, D. C. — Ruth Safran, Deputy Information Officer; Marcella Slajchert, Public Information Officer. Also Helen Matousek, Director, UNRRA Division of Training, United States Zone of Germany; Vaclav Josef Vondracek, Research Officer in Child Search and Czechoslovakian Red Cross. And Mrs. G. Larson Sperry, Child Care Consultant, United States Committee for the Care of European Children. *United Nations International Children's Emergency (or Endowment) Fund:* Mrs. Patricia Palmer, Chief of Public Information for Europe; Dolores Pember, Information Section. *United Nations Educational, Scientific, and Cultural Organization:* Gerald L. Carnes, UNESCO Liaison Officer, Lake Success; William Farr, Deputy Director, Mass Communications Department, UNESCO House, Paris, France. And Ritchie Calder, member of the United Kingdom National Commission for UNESCO, and Science Editor the London *News Chronicle. World Health Organization:* Dr. Martha M. Eliot, Assistant Director-General, Geneva, Switzerland; Roberto Rendueles, Public Information Officer, Lake Success.

IN THE UNITED STATES GOVERNMENT   *Department of Agriculture:* Gertrude L. Warren, Organization of 4-H Club Work, Extension Service. *Department of State, the United States National Commission for UNESCO:* Howard F. Vickery, Assistant Director, UNESCO Relations Staff; Mrs. Mary D. Mack, Information Officer; Herbert Spielman, Special Assistant to George D. Stoddard. *Federal Security Agency, Office of Education:* Nora E. Beust, Specialist for School and Children's Libraries.

EDUCATORS   Leonard S. Kenworthy, Department of Education, Brooklyn College, Brooklyn, New York; Albert Hoefer, 4-H Clubs, New York State Colleges of Agriculture and Home Economics; Alexander J. Stoddard, Superintendent of Schools, Los Angeles, California; Paul Witty, School of Education, Northwestern University, Evanston, Illinois; Ben D. Wood, Professor of Collegiate Educational Research, Columbia University, New York City, New York.

LIBRARIANS   Mildred L. Batchelder, Executive Secretary, Division of Libraries for Children and Young People, American Library Association; Helen S. Carpenter, Acting Director of Libraries, Board of Education, Greater New York; Mrs. Eileen Graves, Periodicals Division, New York Public Library; Della McGregor, Chief, Juvenile Division, St. Paul Public Library, St. Paul, Minnesota; Jean C. Roos, Supervisor, Youth Department, Cleveland Public Library, Cleveland, Ohio; Margaret C. Scoggin, Young People's Specialist, New York Public Library; Mabel L. Williams, Superintendent, Work with Schools, New York Public Library, New York City, New York. Johanna R. Wolff, Children's and Young People's Librarian, Public Library, the Hague, Netherlands.

IN PROFESSIONAL AND VOLUNTARY ORGANIZATIONS   *American Booksellers Association:* Gilbert E. Goodkind, Executive Secretary. *American Friends Service Committee:* Clarence E. Pickett, Executive Secretary; Dorothy Sakasegawa, Director of Public Relations; Barbara W. Moffett, American Section, Public Relations. *American National Red Cross:* Livingston L. Blair, Vice-President for Junior Red Cross and Educational Relations. *Boy Scouts of America:* Elbert K. Fretwell, Chief Scout; W. Arthur McKinney, Assistant to the Chief Scout Executive. *CARE* (Cooperative for American Remittances to Europe): Robert Stanforth, UNESCO Liaison Officer. *Children's Village, Dobbs Ferry, New York:* Mrs. Muriel Lawrence, Director of Public Relations. *Commission on International Education Reconstruction:* Harold E. Snyder, Director; Mrs. Margretta S. Austin. *Doubleday and Company, Inc.:* A. Milton Runyon, Executive Vice-President; Mrs. Alma R. Cardi, Designer-typographer; Ethel M. Ryan, Chief of Copy Editing. *Junior Literary Guild:* Thérèse Doumenjou, Editorial Executive; Mrs. Ruth Clement Hoyer, editor of *Young Wings;* Lee M. Hoffman, Ann Maturi.

UNESCO'S PILOT PROJECT IN MARBIAL VALLEY, HAITI

IN EVERY STATE IN THE
UNITED STATES, SCHOOL
LIBRARIES FEATURE THE
UNITED NATIONS

BIBLIOGRAPHY   In the preparation of this book, in
addition to the publications listed below, we continuously consulted the
United Nations Yearbook, the *Reports of the Secretary-General*, and UN
press releases and radio scripts, on file at the United Nations. United Nations
publications are obtainable in the United States at the International Documents Service, Columbia University Press, 2960 Broadway, New York 27,
N.Y. United States Government publications are obtainable from the Superintendent of Documents, United States Government Printing Office, Washington 25, D.C. Other sources for material are indicated below.

RECOMMENDED FOR ALL SCHOOL
AND YOUNG PEOPLE'S LIBRARIES

UNITED NATIONS PUBLICATIONS

BASIC FACTS ABOUT THE UNITED NATIONS. A convenient manual of current information about the United Nations and its related agencies. 15¢

LITTLE ARAB GIRL WAITS FOR HER PORTION OF UNICEF FOOD IN ISRAEL

THE CHARTER OF THE UNITED NATIONS AND THE STATUTE OF THE INTERNATIONAL COURT OF JUSTICE. 10¢

EVERYMAN'S UNITED NATIONS. A popularly written handbook containing a résumé of United Nations work to date. $1.50

FOOD AND PEOPLE. Series of six booklets; complete set with Discussion Guide. $1.65

GUIDE TO THE UNITED NATIONS CHARTER. An illustrated booklet describing how the Charter came into being and how its various provisions have been put into operation. 50¢

OUR RIGHTS AS HUMAN BEINGS. A discussion guide to the Declaration of Human Rights. Contains the text of the Declaration. 10¢

UNESCO COURIER. A lively, fully illustrated periodical containing news of UNESCO activities. Annual subscription, $1.50

UNITED NATIONS STUDY KIT #1. A careful selection of current booklets, pamphlets, etcetera, designed to provide an introduction to the United Nations and the Specialized Agencies. $1.00

UNITED NATIONS BULLETIN. Published twice monthly by the UN Department of Public Information and presenting a comprehensive review of the activities of the UN and its related agencies. Annual subscription, $4.50

UNITED STATES GOVERNMENT PUBLICATIONS

BUILDING ROADS TO PEACE. The exchange of people between the United States and other countries. 25¢

PATTERNS OF COOPERATION. Achievements of international organizations in the economic and social field. 50¢

THE UNESCO STORY. A resource and action booklet for organizations and communities in the United States. 55¢

MISCELLANEOUS PUBLICATIONS

HOW PEOPLES WORK TOGETHER. An illustrated account of the aims and functions of the United Nations and its related agencies. 50¢ (Obtainable from Manhattan Publishing Company, 255 Lafayette Street, New York 12, N. Y.)

UNITED NATIONS REPORTER. An eight-page monthly review of current UN activities, prepared especially for the use of organizations and students. Annual subscription, $1.00. Special rates for bulk subscriptions. (Obtainable from James Gray, Inc., 216 East 45th Street, New York 17, N. Y.)

GENERAL REFERENCES

UNITED NATIONS PUBLICATIONS

BUILDING FOR PEACE: The Story of the First Four Years of the United Nations, 1945-1949

CATALOGUE OF ECONOMIC AND SOCIAL PROJECTS. March 1949

CHART: FUNCTIONS OF THE SPECIALIZED AGENCIES

E.C.E. IN ACTION: The Story of the United Nations Economic Commission for Europe

ECONOMIC AND SOCIAL COUNCIL REPORT. August 30, 1948—August 15, 1949

FILM STRIPS AND MOTION PICTURES, Bibliography

TECHNICAL ASSISTANCE FOR ECONOMIC DEVELOPMENT

UNITED NATIONS CONFERENCE ON INTERNATIONAL ORGANIZATION. San Francisco, 1945

UNITED NATIONS DAY, OCTOBER 1949: World-wide Messages and Observances

WHAT THE UNITED NATIONS IS DOING FOR THE NON-SELF-GOVERNING TERRITORIES

UNITED STATES GOVERNMENT PUBLICATIONS

ECONOMIC AND SOCIAL PROBLEMS IN THE UNITED NATIONS

INTERNATIONAL TRADE ORGANIZATION: Key to Expanding World Trade and Employment

KOREA, 1945—1948

QUESTIONS AND ANSWERS ABOUT THE UNITED NATIONS

STRENGTHENING THE FORCES OF FREEDOM: Speeches and Statements of Secretary of State Acheson

TECHNIQUE FOR PEACE, the United Nations and Pacific Settlement, by James N. Hyde

THE UNITED NATIONS—FOUR YEARS OF ACHIEVEMENT

UNITED STATES PARTICIPATION IN THE UNITED NATIONS: Report by the President to Congress for the Year 1948

UNITED STATES POLICY IN THE KOREAN CRISIS

MISCELLANEOUS PUBLICATIONS

FREEDOM'S CHARTER: The Universal Declaration of Human Rights, by O. Frederick Nolde. Foreign Policy Association

SECURITY OF THE UNITED STATES AND WESTERN EUROPE. American Association for the United Nations

TEACHING UNITED NATIONS: A Pictorial Report. National Education Association of the United States

TOWARD FREEDOM FROM WANT. Handbook on the United Nations, by Anne Winslow.

American Association for the United Nations

UNITED NATIONS GUARDS AND TECHNICAL FIELD SERVICES. American Association for the United Nations

UNITED NATIONS NEWSLETTER. Published monthly, $1.00 a year. Obtainable from James Gray, Inc.

"WE THE PEOPLE . . .". A Brief History of the United Nations. American Association for the United Nations

FAO

UNITED NATIONS PUBLICATIONS

FAO COMMODITY REPORTS
FAO NEWSLETTER. Monthly bulletin
PROGRAM FOR THE 1950 WORLD CENSUS OF
AGRICULTURE
REPORTS OF THE DIRECTOR-GENERAL OF FAO,
1948, 1949
REPORT OF THE FAO MISSION TO GREECE
THE STATE OF FOOD AND AGRICULTURE: Annual

Survey of World Conditions and Prospects,
1948, 1949
THE STORY OF FAO
THIEVES OF STORED GRAIN
TRAINING RURAL LEADERS. Shantan Bailie
School, Kansu Province, China
UNASYLVA: FAO International Review of For-
estry and Forest Products
WORLD OF PLENTY

UNITED STATES GOVERNMENT PUBLICATIONS

THE POINT FOUR PROGRAM

UNITED STATES AGRICULTURE IN THE WORLD
FOOD SITUATION

MISCELLANEOUS PUBLICATIONS

The Rotarian, May, 1950 — "Pioneers — 1950
Variety," by William F. McDermott

*Specific quotation credit: New York Times
Magazine,* October 2, 1949 — "Hoes and
Show-How Come First," by Norris E. Dodd

IRO

UNITED NATIONS PUBLICATIONS

CONVENTION ON GENOCIDE
FACTS ABOUT REFUGEES
FORGOTTEN ELITE

HUMAN RIGHTS AND GENOCIDE
INTERNATIONAL REFUGEE ORGANIZATION, 1948-
1949
IRO NEWS REPORTS, Monthly bulletin

UNITED STATES GOVERNMENT PUBLICATIONS

DISPLACED PERSONS COMMISSION: Report to the President and the Congress, February 1, 1949

MISCELLANEOUS PUBLICATIONS

ORPHANS OF THE STORM: Bulletin U. S. Committee for the Care of European Children

UNESCO

UNITED NATIONS PUBLICATIONS

A CHILD NAMED MARIKA
A SCHOOLBELL IN THE WILDERNESS
ART MUSEUMS IN NEED
BOOK OF NEEDS NUMBER 1; NUMBER 2
CHILDREN'S COMMUNITIES
GOING TO SCHOOL IN WAR-DEVASTATED COUN-
TRIES
HOMELESS CHILDREN
IMPETUS. A monthly review
INTERNATIONAL FELLOWSHIPS
IT'S YOURS FOR THE GIVING
LIBRARIES IN NEED
MISSION TO HAITI
ORGANIZING INTERNATIONAL VOLUNTARY WORK
CAMPS

QUARTERLY BULLETIN OF FUNDAMENTAL EDU-
CATION
REPORTS OF THE DIRECTOR-GENERAL
SCIENCE LIAISON
SCIENCE MUSEUMS IN NEED
STUDY ABROAD
THE TEACHER AND THE POST-WAR CHILD IN
WAR-DEVASTATED COUNTRIES, by Leonard
S. Kenworthy
THIS IS OUR POWER: Speeches by Julian Huxley
and Jaime Torres Bodet
TOWARDS WORLD UNDERSTANDING: A Series of
Booklets for Teachers
UNESCO A WORLD PROGRAMME
UNESCO IN ACTION: Seminar for International
Understanding, 1947

UNITED STATES GOVERNMENT PUBLICATIONS

GENERAL CONFERENCE: Report of the United
States Delegation at Second Session of the
UNESCO General Conference
KANSAS STORY ON UNESCO
REPORT OF THE UNITED STATES TO THE UNITED
NATIONS ON TEACHING ABOUT THE UNITED
NATIONS IN THE EDUCATIONAL INSTITU-
TIONS OF THE UNITED STATES
UNESCO AND YOU: Questions and Answers on

the What and Why of Your Share in
UNESCO
UNESCO TODAY: An Informal Report on UNESCO
and the U. S. National Commission for
UNESCO
UNITED STATES NATIONAL COMMISSION UNESCO
NEWS: Monthly Bulletin
WORLD UNDERSTANDING BEGINS WITH CHILDREN,
by Delia Goetz

MISCELLANEOUS PUBLICATIONS

A BETTER WORLD: Manual of Suggestions for
the Presentation of the UN in the Elementary and Junior High School Years.
Board of Education, City of New York

CARE BOOK PROGRAM, CARE, 20 Broad Street,
New York 5, N. Y.
THE CHILDREN'S VILLAGE. Children's Village,
Dobbs Ferry, N. Y.

CIER HANDBOOK, First and second editions. Commission for International Educational Reconstruction, Washington, D. C.

CITIZENS AT WORK, American Friends Service Committee Bulletin

EDUCATION FOR ONE WORLD, 1949-50: Annual Census of Foreign Students in the United States. Institute of International Education

FRIENDLY SERVICE IN MEXICO, American Friends Service Committee

IN OUR HANDS: Work Camps and Community Service Units. American Friends Service Committee

INVEST YOUR SUMMER: Catalogue of Service Opportunities Prepared by the Commission on Youth Service Projects for the United Christian Youth Movement

LET'S FACE THE FACTS AND ACT! Curriculum Bulletin for Elementary Schools. St. Paul, Minnesota, Board of Education

PIERRE CERESOLE. American Friends Service Committee

THE S IN UNESCO. Los Angeles, California, Board of Education

THE UNITED NATIONS: YOU AND OTHERS: Curriculum Bulletin for Junior High Schools. St. Paul, Minnesota, Board of Education.

UNESCO BULLETIN FOR PRINCIPALS, DIRECTORS, AND SUPERVISORS. Los Angeles, California, Board of Education

Specific quotation credits: The Horn Book, January, 1950—"The Outlook Tower," by Margaret C. Scoggin; *The Junior League Magazine,* March, 1950—"Pick and Shovel Diplomats," by Leta Cromwell; *The News Chronicle,* London, 1949—"Men Against the Desert" series, by Ritchie Calder.

UNICEF

UNITED NATIONS PUBLICATIONS

FACTS ABOUT UNICEF

FOR THE CHILDREN

REPORT ON CHILD NUTRITION: Prepared by Joint FAO and WHO Committee

TO THE CHILDREN FROM THE UNITED NATIONS

UNICEF: A Compendium of Information, June, 1950

UNICEF AT WORK

THE WORK OF UNICEF: Statement Made to the General Assembly, May, 1949

WHO

UNITED NATIONS PUBLICATIONS

CHRONICLE OF THE WORLD HEALTH ORGANIZATION. Monthly publication.

THIRD WORLD HEALTH ASSEMBLY, May 8, 1950: Information Folder Prepared for Press and Radio Correspondents

WHO NEWSLETTER. Monthly publication

WORLD WAR ON TUBERCULOSIS

UNITED STATES GOVERNMENT PUBLICATIONS

A NEW LOOK AT CHILD HEALTH, by Brock Chisholm

WORLD HEALTH ORGANIZATION: PROGRESS AND PLANS

MISCELLANEOUS PUBLICATIONS

Specific quotation credit: Collier's, January 28, 1950 — "The U. N.'s Merciful War, by David Perlman

BOOKS

AROUND THE WORLD IN ST. PAUL, by Alice L. Sickels, University of Minnesota Press

HOW THE UNITED NATIONS WORKS, by Tom Galt, Thomas Y. Crowell Company

PEACE ON EARTH, by Trygve Lie, Jaime Torres Bodet, John Boyd-Orr, Ralph Bunche, Benjamin Cohen, Herbert V. Evatt, Eleanor Roosevelt, and others. Hermitage House

THE SILENT BILLION SPEAK, by Frank C. Laubach. The Friendship Press

THE TASK OF THE NATIONS, by Herbert V. Evatt. Duell, Sloan and Pearce

YOU AND THE UNITED NATIONS, by Lois Fisher. The Children's Press

EXPECTANT LOOKS AS YEMENITE CHILDREN AT EIN
SHEMER REFUGEE CAMP LINE UP FOR UNICEF RATIONS

WRITING THE LATEST
UN NEWS FOR THEIR
SCHOOL PAPER
IN LOS ANGELES

INDEX

Agricultural organizations, youth, 77–78

All-India Institute of Hygiene and Public Health, Calcutta, 74

Allied Armies of Occupation, aiding refugees, 21

American Bookseller's Association, book coupon plan, 167

American Catholic Committee for Refugees, finding homes for DP's, 33

American Friends Service Committee: starving youth in Europe aided, 52; UNESCO-sponsored schools for Arabs, 127

American Library Association, 164

Ammundsen, Dr. Esther, BCG teams organized, 64

Andreassen, Else, BCG team, 61–62

Arab refugees, UNESCO sponsored schools, 127–9

Arolsen, Germany, International Tracing Service headquarters, 26

Atlantic Charter, Four Freedoms, 154, 186

Australia, DP groups welcomed, 28

Bacillus Calmette Guerin (BCG), tuberculosis campaign, 62–68

Batchelder, Mildred, 164

BCG. See Bacillus Calmette Guerin

Beirut, Lebanon, UNESCO General Conference (1949), 127

Belgium, DP's welcomed, 28, 33

Belios, Dr. George, malaria control in India, 104–5

Better World, A, UN school curriculum plan, 154

Beust, Nora, 164

Bill of Rights, American, 184

Bocobo, Mrs. Dulce L., Nutrition Officer for FAO, 88

Bodet, Jaime Torres, illiteracy campaign, 174; quoted, 146, 155

Book Week, United States, 163

Books: coupon plan, 167; book traffic blocks, 166

Boy Scouts, International Bureau: DP's aided, 25–26; starving European youth aided, 52; UNESCO affiliation, 120

UNICEF SUPPLIES GO BY PACK TRAIN IN THE MOUNTAINS

Boyd-Orr, Lord, *quoted*, 80

Boys Town, Italy, 131–33, 135

Braille, Louis, alphabet for the blind, 167

Braille Conference, International, 168

Brazil, DP groups welcomed, 28

Briggs, Elizabeth, 164

Bundesrealgymnasium, Vienna, adopted by American school, 123–27

Buntzen, John, BCG team, *quoted*, 66–67

Calder, Ritchie, Arid Regions research, 149; *quoted*, 150

Canada, DP groups welcomed, 28

CARE (Cooperative for American Remittances to Europe): packages supplemented by UNICEF, 56; starving European youth aided, 52

Ceresole, Pierre, International Work Camps, 138–39

Child, National Committee for the Protection of, Honduras, 72

Child Search Bureau, Esslingen, Germany, 18, 26–27

Child Search Teams, accomplishments, 34

Children: concentration camp prisoners, 25; kidnaped from Lidice, 19–21; "unaccompanied," 24

Children, War's Victims—The Education of the Handicapped (UNESCO publication), 122

Children's Bureau, Washington, represented on Nutrition Committee, 51

Children's Center, Paris, 74

Children's Communities: A Way of Life for War's Victims (UNESCO publication), 135

Children's Communities, International Federation of, 136

Children's Village, Dobbs Ferry, New York, 136–38

Chisholm, Dr. Brock, Director-General WHO, 97; *quoted*, 107

Cholera epidemic, Egypt, 95

CIER. *See* Commission for International Educational Reconstruction

Colour Reproductions (UNESCO publication), 158

Commission for International Educational Reconstruction (CIER), 122; —UNESCO Commission partnership, 123

Concentration camps: child prisoners, 25; Lidice women, 18

Constitution of the United States, Amendments, 184

Corti, Walter, Pestalozzi Village, 134

County agents, advisors to 4-H Club members, 78, 81

Cromwell, Leta, Work Camps, *quoted*, 140–42

Currency, "soft" and "hard," 166–67

Cuvelier, Marcel, *Jeunesses Musicales*, 159

Dawes, J. C., sanitation survey, 100–1

Declaration of Independence, American, 181–82

Declaration of the Rights of Man, French, 182

Disney, Walt: films, popularity of, 72; hookworm motion picture, 172

Displaced Persons (DP's): Boy Scouts, 25–26; centers constructed for housing, 22; Hard Core (unwanted), 32–33; homes, finding for, 22–23, 27–28; IRO, co-operation with, 24; physically handicapped, 33; record cards, 24; teachers in schools, 24; town groups organized, 24; "unaccompanied," 24; *see also* International Refugee Organization

Dodd, Norris E., *quoted*, 89, 90–91

Don Suisse, organization, 52, 132, 133

DP's. *See* Displaced Persons

Economic and Social Council, permanent Specialized Agencies, 40–41

Education, Allied Ministers, meeting in London, 116

Egypt, cholera epidemic, 95

Eisenhower, Milton D., school textbooks, 155

Eliot, Dr. Martha, survey of undernourished children, 51–52

Eloesser, Dr. Leo, WHO mission to China, 101

Emancipation Declaration (Abraham Lincoln), 182

Epidemic Control Station, Geneva, 95

European Children, Committee for the Care of, 30

European Forestry and Forestry Products Commission, 86

Evans, Luther H., *quoted*, 167

FAO. *See* Food and Agriculture Organization

Farm Youth Exchange plan, international, 78

Farmers' Clubs, Junior, 78

Fellowes, G. G., Loyalty School UN work, 152–53

Finn, Dr. Donovan J., FAO Fisheries Division, 86

Finnerty, John, mayor of Children's Village, 136–38

5-S Club, India, 78

Flanagan, Father Edward Joseph, aid to Italian boys, 132

Flint, Hilde, school adoption plan, 123–24

Food and Agriculture Organization (FAO): charter, 79; development, 79–81; disaster help, 107; fellowships, 82; fisheries, 85–86; foreign government co-operation, 82; forestry products, 86; government teams, 82–91; Greece, mission in, 103; insect pest control, 85; livestock feeding, 80; missions, work

Food and Agriculture Organization *(cont.)*

of, 84–85; motto, 79; nutritionists, 87; plant scientists, 81; regional offices, 81; rice production, 86–87; rinderpest vaccine, 86; Science Offices, Field, 149; seed problems, 81; seeds and plants, two-way traffic, 82; setup, 80; soil conservation conference in Italy, 85; technical assistance fund, share of, 90; timber cutting, 80; UNICEF, long-range plans, 71; WHO partnership, 98

Food and People (UNESCO publication), 152

Food and the Family (Mead), 152

Forestry, Latin-American Conference, 86

Forestry and Timber Utilization Conference, 86

Four Freedoms, Atlantic Charter, 154, 186

4-H Clubs: food, world production, 152; motto, 79; purpose, 77

Fundamental Education, UNESCO partnership with FAO and WHO, 174

Future Farmers, food, world production, 152

Genetic Stocks, The FAO Catalogue of, 82

Geography in International Understanding, 155

George, William R., George Junior Republic, 133

Gettysburg Address (Abraham Lincoln), *quoted,* 182

Girl Guides, starving European youth aided, 52

Girl Scouts: DP's aided, 25; starving European youth aided, 52; UNESCO affiliation, 120

Gorgi, Habib, Egyptian children's art exhibit, 157–58

Great Britain, DP groups welcomed, 28

Greece: dietary deficiencies, 88–89; malaria control, 103; nutrition service, 89

Greece, Report of the FAO Mission for, 84

Haiti, Marbial Valley project, 170–76

Hambridge, Gove, *quoted,* 91

Health Service, National, Denmark, BCG field teams, 63

Help-for-Europe organizations, Norway, BCG field teams, 63

"Hoes and 'Show-How' Come First" (Dodd) *quoted,* 90

Holsapple, Kathryn C., school adoption plan, 123, 127

Homeless Children (UNESCO publication), 135

Human Rights, Declaration of, 176, 181; exhibits, 154

Human Rights Commission of the UN, 179–81

Humburska, Miluse, BCG team, 61–62

Huxley, Julian, Director-General UNESCO, 115

Illiteracy, international campaign against, 178–74

Immaculate Conception Home, Lodi, New Jersey, DP family welcomed, 33

India, malaria control, 104–5

Indo-Pacific Fisheries Council, 85

Influenza Center, World, 107

Insect control campaigns, 103–5, 107

International Refugee Organization (IRO): accomplishments, 22–24, 34; camp in Frankfort, 21; DP teen-agers, sending to new homes, 28–30; DP's, finding new homes for, 27–28; embarkation centers, 28–30; establishing, 21, 22; financial support, 22; foreign governments' co-operation, 22; staff, 23; functions, 41; *see also* Displaced Persons

International Relations Clubs, 124, 152

International Tracing Service (ITS), 18; accomplishments, 34; headquarters at Arolsen, Germany, 26

IRO. *See* International Refugee Organization

Italy, WHO Survey Mission, 100

ITS. *See* International Tracing Service

Janitschek, Dr. Norbert, school adoption plan, 124

Julien, Henri: holiday camp at Moulin Vieux, 136; *République d'Enfants,* 136

Junior Music groups, 159; international congress, 159–60

Keller, Helen, *quoted,* 168

Kenworthy, Leonard S., UNESCO booklet, 117–19

Kingsley, J. Donald, DP's, finding homes for, 28, 33–34

Koch, Dr. Robert, discoverer of tuberculin, 62

Kruger, Pit, international hostel, 133

Labour Organization of the UN, International, Work Camp projects, 142

LaGuardia, Fiorello, UNICEF proposed, 38

Laksmanan, Dr. C. K., report on Asia, 70

Laubach, Frank C., reading charts, 174

Lebensborn Homes, Nazi, 19

LeLièvre, Paul, boys' farm community, 133

Lepman, Mrs. Jella, Munich library plan, 164–65

Let's Face the Facts and Act, UN school curriculum plan, 154

Libraries, special, UNESCO sponsored, 164

Libraries in Need (UNESCO publication), 122

Library, International Youth, Munich, Germany, 164–66

Library Associations, International Federation of, 164

Lidice, Czechoslovakia: children kidnaped, disposition of, 19; destruction by Nazis, 18

Lie, Trygve, background, 42–44

Lincoln, Abraham: Emancipation Declaration, 182; Gettysburg Address, *quoted,* 182

Lincoln, Dr. Edith Maas, *quoted,* 106

Lions Club, International, starving European youth aided, 52

Louis Pasteur Junior High School, adopts Viennese school, 123–27

Loyalty School, Alberta, Canada, model Security Council meeting, 152–53

Lund, Dr., BCG team, 61–62

MacKenzie, Sir Clutha, Braille script, universal, 168; *quoted,* 168

Magna Charta, English, 181

Malaria Campaign, International, Greece, 103

Marika, the Fate of 340,000 *Greek Children* (UNESCO publication), 122

Mead, Margaret, of American Museum of Natural History, author of *Food and the Family,* 152

Medical Science Congresses, Congress of, 98

Men Against the Desert (Calder), 150

Metraux, Dr. Alfred, Marbial Valley project, Haiti, 171

Milk bars, setting up in Europe, 53

Millet, Dr. Jean Michel, BCG team, 68

Monnet, J. R., DP Boy Scout troops, organizing, 25–26

Music, International Council of, 159

Music Fund, International, 159

Musicales, Jeunesses, 159

Nazis: Lebensborn Homes, 19; Lidice, destruction, 18; Norway, invasion, 43; slave laborers, child, 33

Needs, Books of (UNESCO publication), 120, 122

New Education Fellowship, 135

New Life (mimeographed newspaper of DP United States Reception Center), 31

New Utrecht High School, Brooklyn, school supplies sent to Holland, 123

New Zealand, DP teen-agers welcomed, 28

Norway: blind DP's welcomed, 33; Nazi invasion, 43

Nounih, Fattah, request for school bell, 129

Nutrition, Institute of, Manila, 88

Nutrition Committee, members, 51

Ording, Aake, UN Appeal for Children, 38

Organizations, voluntary, aiding starving in Europe, 52

Pais Clubs, Argentina, 78

Palestine, UNESCO-sponsored schools for Arab refugees, 127–29

Pan-American Sanitary Bureau, 95, 96

Parent-Teacher Association, school adoption plan, 126

Parran, Dr. Thomas, Asia, report on, 70

Pate, Maurice, UNICEF, organizing, 42

Pellet, Dr. Max, BCG team, 68

Perlman, David, interview with Dr. George Belios, *quoted,* 104–5

Pestalozzi Village, Trogen, Switzerland, youth community, 134–35

Philippines, dietary deficiencies, 87–88

"Pick and Shovel Diplomats" (Cromwell), *quoted,* 140–42

Pilot Project, Marbial Valley, Haiti, 170

Popular Association of Hungarian Youth, school-building brigades, 120

Pro Juventute, Swiss Youth Organization, 134

Reception Center, Bronx, New York, caring for DP children, 30–31

Red Crescent, organization, starving European youth aided, 52

Red Cross, International: cholera epidemic in Egypt, 95–96; disaster help, 107; prisoners-of-war program, 42; refugees, aiding, 21; starving European youth aided, 52; UNESCO affiliation, 120; UNESCO-sponsored schools for Arabs, 127

Red Cross, Junior, gift boxes for schools abroad, 123

Red Cross, Scandinavian, tuberculosis campaign, 62–63

Refugees: Arab, 127; European, 21–22; *see also* Displaced Persons; International Refugee Organization

Refuse, Domestic, The Storage, Collection and Disposal of, in the U.S.A. (Dawes), 100–1

Rice Commission, International, 87

Rogers, Helen Jewett, school adoption plan, 124

Roos, Jean, head of Cleveland Public Library's Robert Louis Stevenson Room, 164

Roosevelt, Franklin Delano: FAO, beginning of, 79; Four Freedoms message, 154

Rotary Club, International, starving European youth aided, 52

Royaumont, L'Abbaye de, France, Work Campers' conference, 143

Saumagne, Charles, Arid Regions research, 150

Scheele, Dr. Leonard A., sanitation survey, United States, 100; *quoted,* 101

Schoolbell in the Wilderness, A (UNESCO publication), 129

Schools: adoption through UNESCO, 123–24; DP teachers, 24; Feeding Demonstration Centers, 87–88; studying UN Charter, 153–54

Science Clubs, 145–47

Science Liaison (UNESCO publication), 149

Scoggin, Margaret C., *quoted*, 165–66

Sea, International Council for the Exploration of, 85

Serum Institute, Copenhagen, Denmark: BCG field teams, 63; BCG vaccine, 64

Service Civil International, International Work Camp, 139

Simon, Dr. Claud, BCG team, 68

Snyder, Harold E., educational survey, Greece, 117, 122

Stankevic, Dr. Kristini, 74

Stoddard, Alexander J., UNESCO city schools organization plan, 123

Study Abroad (UNESCO publication), 74

Sweden, DP teen-agers welcomed, 28

Switzerland, international village for youth community, 134–35

Sztehlo, Pastor, youth community, 133

Teacher and the Post-War Child in War-Devastated Countries, The (UNESCO publication), 118

Teen Town, British Zone, Germany, 25

Textbooks, school, 155–56

Theatre Institute, International, 160

Theatre Month, International, 160

Totalitarian states, interest, 180

Truman, Harry S., *quoted*, 90

Tsongas, Andromache, FAO Nutritionist in Greece, 88–89

Tuberculosis: BCG vaccine, 62; control, 63–68, 106

Tuck, William Hallam, Director-General IRO, 22

"Turning Point in the World Food Situation, The" (Dodd), *quoted*, 89

UNESCO. *See* United Nations Educational, Scientific and Cultural Organization

UNESCO Courier, The, 147

UNESCO Day program, London, 152

UNESCO House, Paris: composers' night, 159; international headquarters of information, 115, 120; painting reproductions exhibition, 157, 158; Science Clubs at work, 146; Theatre Institute, International, 160

UNESCO Story, The, 156

UNESCO Thinkers' Club, charter, 156

UNICEF. *See* United Nations International Children's Emergency Fund

United Nations: Human Rights Commission, 179–80; declaration, 181; school curriculum plans, 154

United Nations Appeal for Children, 38; countries contributing, 40

United Nations Bulletin, quoted, 89

United Nations Charter: human rights, references to, 185; pledge to youth, 17

United Nations Educational, Scientific and Cultural Organization (UNESCO): activities, 122; Arid Regions research, 149–50; Art Committee, 158, 159; book coupon plan, 167; book traffic blocks, 166; charter, 115; Children's Communities, International Federation of, 136; CIER partnership, 122–23; currency, "soft" and "hard," 166–67; educational reconstruction, 115–16; Egyptian art exhibit, 157, 158; fellowships, 136, 163; Fundamental Education, 174; Human Rights declaration exhibits, 154; illiteracy, international campaign against, 173; libraries, aid to, 164; Marbial Valley project, Haiti, 170–76; Music, International Council, 159; National Commissions, 115, 122, 159; poster and essay contest, 158; publications, 118, 120, 122, 129, 135, 142, 149, 152, 158, 176; reconstruction money, 122; school and class adoption, 123–24; school studies, 153; school textbooks, 155; schools for Arab refugees, 127–29; Science Clubs, 145–47; Science Offices, Field, 149; scientific abstracting, 148; teachers' booklet, 114–19; technical assistance fund, share of, 90; WHO partnership, 98; Work Camp Co-ordinating Committee, 142; Work Camps, International, 139–43; youth communities, 134; Youth Community Conference, Trogen, Switzerland, 134, 135; youth meeting at Moulin Vieux, 136

United Nations International Children's Emergency (Endowment) Fund (UNICEF): Arab refugees, aid to, 57; Asia, aid to, 70–71; Christmas card, 56; clothing supply shipments, 56; disaster help, 107; disease, fight against, 72; established, 38–40; feeding centers, demonstration, 72; feeding stations, 53, 68; fellowships, 74; food program, 50–54, 70–71; foreign governments' co-operation, 38, 51–52; functions, 41; health habits taught, 72; health workers trained, 74; hospitals for youth, 72; insect-control campaign of WHO, 105; letters of appreciation, 58–59; long-range plans, 70–75; meals served, 53, 54; name changed, and organization made permanent, 75; partnership with UN Specialized Agencies, 40–41, 75, 97; poster designs by children, 54–56; school-feeding demon-

United Nations International Children's Emergency (Endowment) Fund (UNICEF) *(cont.)*

stration centers, 87–88; skim-milk powder processing plants in Europe, 72; transportation difficulties, 53; tuberculosis campaigns, 62–68; "UNICEF" a new word, 54

United Nations Relief and Rehabilitation Administration (UNRRA): refugees returning to their homes, 22; setting up, 21–22

United Nations Relief for Palestine Refugees, 57

United Nations Secretariat, 42

United Nations Secretary-General, functions, 42

United Nations Success Story, radio program, 127

United Nations: You and Others, school curriculum plan, 154

United States, DP teen-agers welcomed, 28

United States Department of Agriculture: county agents, 78; Farm Youth Exchange plan, 78

United States Public Health Service: activities, 97, 100; represented on **Nutrition** Committee, 51

UNRRA. *See* United Nations Relief and Rehabilitation Administration

Vine, Dr. James, malaria control in Greece, 103

Visendas, Don Guido, Boys Town, Italy, 131–33, 135

Voices of UNESCO—One Song—One Dance—One World, dramatic festival, 160

Waksman, Dr. Selman A., streptomycin discovered, 67

Washburne, Dr. Carleton, youth communities, 135

WHO. *See* World Health Organization

Wolff, Johanna Rebecca, Netherland's UNESCO fellow's visit to United States, 160–64

Work Camps, International, 139–43

Work Camps, Organizing International Voluntary (UNESCO publication), 142

World Food Council, 80

World Health Assembly, Rome, 97, 100, 102

World Health Organization (WHO): constitution, 97; disaster help, 107; diseases of childhood, 98; drug standardization, 98; epidemic control, 96; established, 97; FAO partnership, 98; fellowships, 106; Geneva headquarters, 98; health surveys, 100; influenza research, 107; insect control, 105, 107; malaria control, 103–5, 107; medical workers, training, 101, 106; nurses, training, 98; rabies, combating, 107; technical assistance fund, share of, 90; tuberculosis control, 62–68, 106; UNESCO partnership, 98; UNICEF partnership, 97; UNICEF long-range plans, 71; whooping-cough control, 107

World Understanding Begins with Children (Goetz), 154

Wright, Daniel E., malaria control in Greece, 103

Yaws, skin disease of rural tropics, 70, 72, 171

Young Farmers' Organization, 77

Young Men's Christian Association: DP's aided, 25; Farm Service Force, 152; starving European youth aided, 52

Young Women's Christian Association: DP's aided, 25; starving European youth aided, 52

Youth Chapters, world food production, 152

Youth communities, 25, 133–38

Youth Hostels movement, 120

Youth organizations, international, aid to DP's, 25

Yugoslavia, BCG team report, 66–67

GUATEMALA INDIANS TRANSPORT

UNICEF SUPPLIES TO A REMOTE VILLAGE

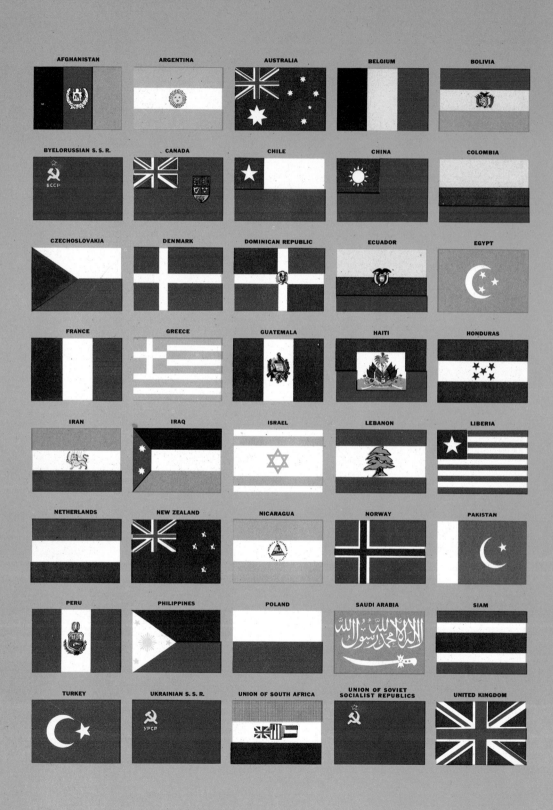